Penguin Books

SHARING THE COUNTRY

Father Frank Brennan is both a Jesuit priest and lawyer. He is the Aboriginal affairs consultant to the Catholic bishops of Australia, legal adviser to the Queensland Aboriginal Co-ordinating Council and the director of Uniya, a Christian centre for social research and action.

Frank Brennan is the author of a book on the law and order debate in Queensland: *Too Much Order With Too Little Law* and co-author of a book on Aboriginal land rights: *Finding Common Ground*. In 1989 he won the United Nations Association of Australia Media Peace Award for some of the many articles he has written in support of Aboriginal rights.

Other books by Frank Brennan

Too Much Order With Too Little Law

Co-author of:
Finding Common Ground:
An Assessment of the Bases of Aboriginal Land Rights

Sharing the Country

Frank Brennan

Penguin Books

Penguin Books Australia Ltd
487 Maroondah Highway, PO Box 257
Ringwood, Victoria 3134, Australia
Penguin Books Ltd
Harmondsworth, Middlesex, England
Viking Penguin, A Division of Penguin Books USA Inc.
375 Hudson Street, New York, New York 10014, USA
Penguin Books Canada Limited
10 Alcorn Avenue, Toronto, Ontario, Canada M4V 1E4
Penguin Books (N.Z.) Ltd
182–190 Wairau Road, Auckland 10, New Zealand

First published by Penguin Books Australia 199
10 9 8 7 6 5 4 3 2 1
Copyright © Frank Brennan, 1991

Typeset in 10½/12 Andover by Midland Typesetters, Maryborough, Victoria
Made and printed in Australia by Australian Print Group

National Library of Australia
Cataloguing-in-Publication data:
Brennan, Frank, 1954–
Sharing the country.
ISBN 0 14 013867 6.
[1]. Aborigines, Australian - Land tenure. [2] Aborigines, Australian
- Civil rights. [3]. Aborigines, Australian - Government
relations. I. Title.

333.20994

'We have to work out a way of sharing this country.'

Mr Wenten Rubuntja
Chairman, Central Land Council,
Barunga
12 June 1988

Contents

Author's note   ix

Introduction:
UNFINISHED BUSINESS   1

1 THE UNRESOLVED ISSUES   17
    Sovereignty   18
    Land Rights   22
    State Rights   40
    Self-Determination   43
    Compensation   52
    Local Treaties   55

2 TREATY TALK BEFORE 1988   58

3 FROM 1988 TO 2001   80
    'Living Together' in 1988   80
    From Treaty to Instrument of Reconciliation   90

4 THE CLOUDS OF GENEVA   110

The UN Working Group on Indigenous
    Populations   111
ILO Convention 107/169   120
Future Directions   123

5 OVERSEAS ATTEMPTS TO AGREE   128
New Zealand   129
Canada   135

Conclusion:
THE WAY FORWARD TO 2001   148

Notes   168

Author's note

I am not an Aborigine and I do not presume to speak for Aborigines. I am a white Australian who seeks greater reconciliation with the descendants of the traditional owners of this land – a reconciliation based on justice for all Australians, including the descendants and inheritors of those who dispossessed Aborigines and the most recently arrived migrants and refugees who have done no wrong to Aborigines. I write this book hoping that Aborigines might belong again throughout this land; and those of us who are not Aboriginal might belong for the first time without shame.

I dedicate this book to the many Australians who have welcomed me on their land and in their homes during my wanderings of the past decade. I thank particularly the staff of Uniya and of the Department of Law and the Federalism Research Centre in the Research School of Social Sciences at the Australian National University for providing the space to write.

Introduction:

UNFINISHED BUSINESS

9 May 1988: Michael Nelson Tjakamarra stood on the 200 square metre granite mosaic in the forecourt of the new Parliament House. The mosaic, named *Tjurkurpa*, depicts the Dreamtime meeting of Australian animals. Seeing the Parliament as the meeting place for different cultures in this land, Mr Tjakamarra said: 'I designed it for a good purpose. For both black and white.'[1] It was a beautiful clear autumn day in Canberra. The sun was bright, the air crisp, and the vapour trails of the Melbourne–Sydney planes could be seen overhead. Beside him stood Elizabeth II, the Queen of England (and Australia). She had just opened the new Parliament House. It was eighty-seven years to the day since the first Australian Parliament had sat in Melbourne on 9 May 1901.

Michael, an Aboriginal painter from Papunya, had provided the design for the meeting-place mosaic crafted from thousands of pieces of granite by Franco Colussi, William McIntosh and Aldo Rossi. The combined effort of these Aboriginal and migrant Australian artisans was the backdrop for a meeting of cultures from opposite sides of the world – a meeting that has gone on in this land for over 200 years, a meeting marked by alienation of the traditional owners and an uneasy belonging by the new settlers. On the balcony above them were the Members of Parliament and honoured guests. In front of them stood the military parade, every person at attention. By their sides were the chatting locals and a large group of Aboriginal demonstrators and their supporters.

Zena Weekes, a three-year-old Aboriginal girl descended from the Eora tribe whose land was Sydney Cove, slipped through the security cordon and presented the Queen with a posy of flowers wrapped in the unmistakable colours of black, red and gold. There were the customary cries: 'What do we want?' 'Land Rights'. 'When do we want it?' 'Now'. The black Rolls-Royce and the white limousines whisked the dignitaries away to lunch. Kevin Gilbert, a member of the Wiradjuri tribe and an honorary adopted member of the local Ngunawal tribe, claimed Tjakamarra had no right to speak outside his own country where he did not belong and that *Tjurkurpa* was under a holy curse that made it a creative and mystical force for justice and retribution.

Inside the grand new building, Prime Minister Bob Hawke had spoken of the spirits of the past that had inhabited Canberra that, according to one version, means meeting place. Such human spirits had lived in this place for at least 21 000 years. The Queen confined herself to more recent spirits; she was sure that Captain Arthur Phillip 'could never have imagined such an event as this, or the scene before us today'. Her son Charles had reflected on the achievements of Captain Cook and King George III's ministers earlier in the year. At the Opera House, before the tall ships made their way into Sydney Harbour on Australia Day 1988, Prince Charles spoke of Cook's discovery and quest for knowledge. He conceded:

For the original people of this land it must have all seemed very different, and if they should say that their predicament has not yet ended, it would be hard to know how to answer, beyond suggesting that a country free enough to examine its own conscience is a land worth living in, a nation to be envied.

After all the royalty had departed our shores, the politicians settled down to business. The first item in the new Parliament House was to be a resolution moved by the

Prime Minister and seconded by the Leader of the Opposition, acknowledging Aboriginal history in Australia and espousing the special place of Aborigines in the maturing nation. However, the Coalition withdrew its support for any such initiative for reconciliation. Their Shadow Minister for Aboriginal Affairs, Chris Miles, explained that they had decided not to proceed because of the negative community response to radical Aboriginal protests. They felt the resolution would not be positively received in the community and hence would fail to promote reconciliation. Adding insult to injury, he said the recent protests 'had led the general Australian community to see the Aboriginal people as not being interested in good relations with non-Aboriginals'. Bipartisan attempts to bring about reconciliation in 1988 were thus short lived.

In March 1990 the Hawke Government went to the polls and was elected for a record fourth term. On 8 May, as the autumn leaves fell in Canberra for the second time since the opening of the new Parliament House, Governor General Bill Hayden opened the thirty-sixth Parliament. His address was largely dedicated to matters of economic reform. At the end of it, however, he spoke of the Government's continuing commitment to 'a genuine reconciliation with Australia's indigenous people'.[2] After his re-election Mr Hawke had written to Dr John Hewson, the Leader of the Opposition, seeking a bipartisan approach in the development of an instrument of reconciliation. A copy of the letter was sent to every State premier and all Opposition leaders in the States and territories of the Commonwealth, attempting to involve all levels of government and all sides of politics in this national task of reconciliation.

The process of reconciliation and the content of any legal document are the concerns of this book. 'Instrument of reconciliation' is the new political term for the long-awaited Aboriginal treaty. The Hawke Government has moved away from the term 'treaty'; the federal Coalition, now rejecting the underlying philosophy of any treaty, is cautious even about the new term. The Fraser Government, like the Hawke Government, was open to the idea of a treaty with Aborigines. But neither government had or has developed its thinking very far on the matter. The word 'treaty' has come to have a specialised meaning in international law, with the result that the Hawke Government now cautions against its use in international fora to refer to agreements between a sovereign government and its indigenous people. The Government has realised that wide community support and bipartisan political endorsement are needed if any instrument of reconciliation is to bring about the social change that it would promise and symbolise. Bipartisan support is by no means assured.

The starting point for reconciliation must be a consideration of the varied hopes and demands expressed by Aborigines for sovereignty, land rights and self-determination. Each of these terms (like the term 'treaty') opens a Pandora's box of possibilities. For every Aborigine who finds clarity and hope in these terms, there is a cluster of non-Aboriginal Australians who are besieged by fear and clouded in confusion. After an analysis of these terms in chapter 1, chapters 2 and 3 provide a brief review of Australian treaty talk before 1988 and a detailed history of the various initiatives proposed by the Hawke Government. Chapter 4 looks at recent developments in international fora in which Aborigines have participated and chapter 5 reviews the approaches taken recently in New Zealand and Canada. This provides a background for proposals about the process and content of an agreement to be finalised before 1 January 2001, the first centenary of the Australian constitution.

It would be a tragedy if a process of reconciliation for all Australians were abandoned because of misunderstandings about words like 'treaty'. These semantic misunderstandings are presently covering deep differences of understanding of the true place of Aborigines in a society built on parliamentary democracy, the rule of law and federalism.

None of these central tenets of Australia's public institutions rules out special recognition of the place of Aborigines. Aboriginal identity is central, not marginal, to Australian life. Putting semantics to one side, it is necessary to identify what Aborigines want, what is justifiable and what is achievable through the negotiation of any agreement. At the same time, there is no reason why we should expect a unanimous Aboriginal viewpoint.

Indigenous people are inevitably marginalised in the new, post-colonial society of which they find themselves a part, without consultation or consent. They have borne the brunt of colonialism and their descendants have the right to retain land, and a social and political organisation that allows them to preserve their cultural identity, while also being able to participate fully in the broader society. In the post-colonial era, indigenous peoples who survive always face two risks: assimilation and discrimination. They have a right to maintain their own identity and, if it is to occur, their integration into the new society should be as the result of free choice, and at their own pace.

In seeking recognition of Aboriginal social and political organisation, we have to move beyond the primitive notion that assimilation is a precondition for justice for all. Equality is not the same as uniformity. Equality of treatment requires a recognition of differences. Minorities themselves are entitled to demand this recognition so they have the opportunity to develop according to their own specific characteristics. However, there are limits. Even minorities must consider the common good of society and the world community. Any decision that indigenous minorities be integrated into the surrounding culture needs to result from their own guaranteed free choice. The government of the society built on Aboriginal dispossession has a responsibility to provide basic services so that individuals and communities can exercise a realistic choice.

Simplistic notions of equality, such as the idea that Aborigines in Australian society should 'just be like the rest of us' or that 'they shouldn't get special treatment' or 'they won't participate', have to be confronted. Australians still need to be educated to a positive appreciation of the complementary diversity of people. A well-understood pluralism is not contrary to the national interest, nor does it undermine principles of fair play.

Aborigines are not simply a self-identifying group in the community who are in need of welfare assistance. They are not just poor whites. No policy should proceed on that basis. As descendants of the first occupants and as the primary custodians of the Aboriginal culture and heritage, Aborigines have a right to continue the management of their community affairs as autonomously as possible within the Australian nation provided they do not act contrary to the common good nor interfere with the rights of others, and provided all community members are given a realistic choice between their community life and the lifestyle available to other Australians. Though the provision of such choice may require special legal arrangements and extra government resources, the cost is justified and necessary given the history of dispossession of land and kin that was the precondition of the birth of modern Australia. Such arrangements are not unacceptable discrimination. They are a recognition of the legitimate aspirations of those who are most truly Australian.

The ambiguities of the treaty discussion since 1987 have opened a chasm of misunderstanding between the major political parties at a national level. Given the lack of bipartisanship on the treaty in recent years, where do we go from here? Many have spoken of the need for what Fred Chaney described in 1980 as 'arrangements between the national Government and the Aboriginal people of Australia which are consensual in nature and which represent the view of Aboriginal citizens of this country as to what is appropriate'.

The bicentennial year was a salutary lesson to us all. We did not know how to speak meaningfully about ourselves as a nation according Aborigines their due place. The next symbolic moment in Australian history is 1 January 2001, the first centenary of the Australian constitution. So there is time to set up a process for consultation, negotiation and approval. If there are to be any consensual arrangements, which accurately reflect the legitimate aspirations of Aborigines, it will take years for the process and education of the community to come to fruition. It cannot be a matter resolved between the Commonwealth Government and a group of Aboriginal leaders. All levels of government must be involved. Local Aboriginal communities must be part of the process. Indeed the community generally must be actively involved, not simply as spectators waiting to be presented with a *fait accompli*. The major political parties have to be talked back to a bipartisan approach. The parameters of what is desirable and achievable have to be articulated clearly and early in the process. Politically there is no possibility of an 'Aboriginal driven' process without initial parameters being set by our politicians. Although Mr Hawke's various statements in 1988 resulted in confusion among some Aboriginal leaders, the Australian Government has clearly set out how far it is prepared to go in its responses to international initiatives for the recognition of indigenous rights. The choice is not between parameters and no parameters, but between parameters that are declared to the Aboriginal leadership and those that are declared to overseas governments but not declared at home. There are strict limits on what is achievable by this process. No political party wants to wind the clock back 200 years, pretending that the negotiation is between a sovereign Aboriginal nation and a later generation representing unjust colonisers.

The Prime Minister has said that the instrument of reconciliation is to fulfil two conditions: it must say something significant, and be acceptable to the majority of Australians. It is not necessarily to have any legal effect. Presumably there will be a need for bipartisan support, although the Prime Minister has never expressed the Government's intention should the Opposition withdraw all prospect of support.

The Opposition has often cited the treaty proposal as an example of the Government's objectionable approach, which they criticise for 'its resort to highly symbolic gestures in place of a careful and continuing attention to the administration of effective programmes'.[3] However, there is a need for both – symbolic gestures and effective programmes. A case needs to be made for this instrument of reconciliation if it is to attract bipartisan support in the Parliament. To effect this reconciliation, words are not enough. But words are essential, especially words that express our national identity, from its beginnings to its maturity. Mr Warwick Smith, when Shadow Minister for Aboriginal Affairs, described the loss of a bipartisan approach as the loss of 'the broad consensus of the 1970s', adding: 'we recognise it is desirable to achieve this again but it requires a great rebuilding exercise.'[4] There is no reason why a process and an instrument of reconciliation could not be the cornerstone of the rebuilding exercise. However bipartisanship should not be a foil for tailoring Aboriginal aspirations to the lowest common denominator.

Both sides when in government during the past decade have seen the need for some negotiated agreement, which is the icing on the cake for the various programmes necessary to accord Aborigines their proper place in Australian society. There is nothing wrong with symbol provided it matches the reality or at least the well-disposed intention. Our history is marked by the lack of any initial agreement between Aborigines and colonisers and the settlers' disregard for instructions from imperial authorities urging the accommodation of Aboriginal interests. We are yet to reach an agreement acceptable to Aborigines and other Australians, permitting us to draw the line on the wrongs of the past and to commit ourselves to a common future. Some Australians will continue to argue that there is no need for any agreement. Even conceding the desirability of an agreement in 1788, some argue it is too late to put right the wrongs. The case needs to be put for a contemporary agreement, which can assure Aborigines of their place and non-Aborigines of their moral entitlement to continued occupancy in good faith. But this cannot be done by self-interested non-Aborigines denying the facts of history, nor by Aborigines asserting absolute and eternally inalienable property rights. We must strip back inflated political rhetoric that in no way matches political intent or legitimate aspirations. Australia's politicians should by now have the political will and skill, and the Australian public the desire, to set up the process for a just and proper settlement by 2001.

Since 1987 Mr Hawke has spoken many times of the need for 'real and lasting reconciliation and honest negotiation between Aboriginal and non-Aboriginal citizens of this nation, leading to an agreement with the Aboriginal people – a treaty, a compact, call it what you will'.[5] In reply, Mr Howard when Leader of the Opposition threatened to tear up any agreement. Since January 1988 the Coalition has not supported any process involving negotiation and agreement with Aborigines. Howard has argued that, 'while a treaty may give some people a warm inner glow of satisfaction, it cannot and will not result in the development of compassionate and sensible policies so desperately needed to overcome the situation faced by many Aboriginal people'.[6] Lines of division were drawn where none existed when the Coalition was in government.

The Hawke Government, despite its rhetoric, has never proposed a treaty in the international law sense. As an agreement in domestic law, it may not even create any enforceable rights. Hawke has described it as 'an umbrella document providing direction and perspective to all areas of policy, including land rights, self-management, customary laws and recognition of Aboriginal culture and religion'. The treaty 'would not sign away the Governments' responsibilities'; it will be 'a national declaration of shared principles and common commitments'.[7]

The Coalition parties while in opposition have been committed to talking up the legal effects of a treaty so as to discredit the idea; meanwhile Labor in government has been talking it down so as to convince non-Aborigines of its reasonableness. The risk is that Aborigines will see the proposal as a symbolic sham and that Opposition antipathy will undermine the reconciliation an agreement is supposed to effect.

It is 200 years too late for a treaty recognising and protecting indigenous rights that were extinguished or overlooked upon colonisation. It is now impossible to adequately compensate particular groups for loss of particular rights. Many Aborigines are now descendants of the vanquishers as well as the vanquished. Solving a moral conundrum we can appeal to a higher authority whose decisions are respected by all parties or we can call all parties to the table and bring about an acceptable compromise. Otherwise we have to put the matter in the 'too hard' basket contenting ourselves with the absurd thought that the past is past and ought to be forgotten. There is no higher authority we can turn to and Aborigines are at least as entitled as our politicians to play a role in choosing between the latter alternatives. If the treaty proposal is unworkable, we should wait to hear that from Aborigines. If compromise is possible, Aborigines should be equipped to stand on an equal footing with government in a consultative process supervised by an independent council. Aboriginal participation in this process could be a real act of self-determination though admittedly subject to the now inescapable and sufficient qualification that self-determination is to be exercised within the Australian nation.

The present political debate is not about semantics. Rather the ongoing quest for national identity that became a national preoccupation in 1988 has emerged as a real political issue focussed on the question: 'Is there a need for us Australians to reassess our history in a way that changes the present?' The debate about the treaty centres on the place of Aborigines in Australia's future. Aborigines are not simply disadvantaged poor deserving welfare assistance until they can overcome their marginalisation. They are citizens deserving special recognition in the Australian nation, they being the inheritors and custodians of the only culture and tradition unique to our society, they being the descendants of the traditional owners of this land, many of their ancestors having been dispossessed of land and separated from their kin without just cause. If they were to be classed only as the disadvantaged poor, there would be no rationale for a negotiated agreement, whatever it be called.

Many Aborigines are still poor citizens who deserve welfare assistance. They are also disadvantaged, they and their ancestors having been denied equal access to opportunities. Affirmative action programmes that accelerate their access to education, training and employment are warranted. Most Aborigines are also the descendants of those who were dispossessed of their lands without consent nor compensation. Land rights legislation has been necessary to respect and recognise their property rights. Even if they were not poor, disadvantaged or dispossessed, Aborigines would still be entitled to recognition and a special place in Australian legal, political and social processes, as the indigenous people of this land. The primary purpose of any just and recognised agreement among Australians by 2001 is the acknowledgement of our national history which entails guaranteed recognition of the place of Aborigines in the future.

The late Professor Bill Stanner knew enough history to play prophet in the preface of his last published work, *White Man Got No Dreaming*, when he wrote:

What troubles me most is an attitude of mind that could come to prevail amongst white Australians: a feeling of irritation apparently based on a conviction that we are saddled with the responsibility for problems not really of our making, and by their nature probably insoluble. The underlying thought is twofold: no one now alive has hurt the Aborigines or their legitimate interests, and no one contemplates deliberately doing so. Whatever wrongs may have been done in the past are surely long ago and far away – the wrongs inflicted by whites long since dead on Aborigines no longer alive. The thought runs on: the worst that white Australians did to black Australians was to come here at all. That is something which now cannot ever be undone. To argue that every new generation of white Australians must accept a liability to compensate every new generation of Aborigines is simply not an argument from a domain of the real world.

I have argued of course that it is a question of whose reality is to be consulted. I have identified things being done now by us to living Aborigines which are very 'real' indeed. Once admit this proposition as true, and our 'real' position changes.[8]

It is that present reality, the real position, that we must consider. Like all reality, it has a history from which it is inseparable if it is to remain comprehensible. The legal fiction on which this nation was founded in 1788 is still working injustices today – injustices that can be alleviated without causing injustice to others, though at times this may require a new balancing of interests. The alleviation is a national responsibility demanding resolution that could be the basis for future reconciliation.

As we work towards the first centenary of federation, we should be able to define ourselves as a nation owning its past and embracing its future, including that of Aborigines. For they are entitled not only to welfare assistance to deliver them from their poverty but also to special recognition as the inheritors and custodians of the only culture and heritage that are unique to this land. This will require an avoidance of inflated rhetoric and a clear statement of the parameters for negotiation and discussion. The process will go nowhere unless it involves State governments as well as the federal government. It will also require the involvement of Australians who are not Aboriginal. For their part, Aboriginal communities and their leaders on the national stage will have to accept principles that are non-negotiable including the sovereignty of Parliament, equality of treatment and opportunity for all Australians.

There is no one Aboriginal viewpoint, and no one acknowledged Aboriginal leader, and no well-resourced, independent, national Aboriginal agencies. It is impossible therefore for anyone to package *the* Aboriginal perspective. Aborigines and their supporters are still learning to distinguish the three key questions that confront them in a political process dominated by the colonising culture. Those questions are:

1 *What do Aborigines want?*
Only Aborigines can provide the answers to this question. There is no more reason to expect unanimity from them than from our parliamentary representatives. Aborigines need structures and processes so that they can make their own compromises with each other to determine their preferred position on any topic on that national agenda. For those whose descendants were dispossessed and whose tribes were broken up, traditional dispute resolution procedures within their own ranks have often been replaced by the power politics of Aboriginal organisations that to outsiders might simply look like disputes between family factions. Even for those whose relationship with their land and clan remains intact, traditional procedures may require adjustment to deal with the big national questions regarding Aboriginal entitlements.

There is a wide variety of Aboriginal viewpoints of what Aborigines want from contemporary Australia. Some, like Michael Mansell, will not be party to any process that presumes them to be Australian citizens. They claim to be Australian Aborigines rather than Aboriginal Australians subject to the laws and policies of Australian governments. They assert sovereignty thathas never been voluntarily surrendered. They see government talk about reconciliation as a denial of their separate nation status. Like anyone they are entitled to their viewpoint.

Others like Charles Perkins proudly see themselves as part of the Australian nation. He has said that, 'Aboriginal people would do well to consider that, in the coming decade, they can gain benefits for themselves and the nation by playing a more involved role in areas beyond Aboriginal affairs'.

If the Mansell viewpoint enjoyed wide support among Aborigines, there would be no point in government proceeding with any process that accepts Aborigines as citizens seeking recognition, rights and reconciliation under Australian law and through the Australian Government. If, as I suspect, the Perkins view is shown to reflect the aspirations of most Aborigines, there is clearly something to be gained by proceeding.

2 *Having ascertained what Aborigines want, which of their claims are justified?*

Aborigines alone cannot provide the answer to this question. They are not the only experts in political morality. For too long, people have stayed in their ideological corners sprouting inflated rhetoric for and against Aboriginal entitlements. There is a need for reasoned debate about the moral limits of Aboriginal entitlements, determining what justice demands for Aborigines. We must consider what additional rights Aborigines should have under Australian law, not because most Aborigines are poor, disadvantaged or dispossessed, but because they are Aboriginal. Two hundred and four years down the track where so many Aborigines can now proudly claim European or Asian ancestry as well as Aboriginal descent, such entitlements are unlikely to take the form of individual rights enforceable in the courts. But they may be collective entitlements capable of respect and recognition by governments and other citizens. Aboriginal communities should be able to live their lives without being forced to be migrants in a foreign society. All Australians have a right to speak and discuss the justice of these claims.

(3) *Which justifiable Aboriginal claims are politically achievable?*
Given that the political process is still driven by the whitefellas, Messrs Hawke and Hewson remain better positioned than Messrs Mansell and Perkins to answer this question. For too long Aborigines have missed out on their entitlements because there has been insufficient hard-headed political analysis by them of what is achievable whether in Brisbane, Sydney, Canberra or Geneva. Because of their disempowerment, lack of access and resources, Aborigines must find friends in our parliaments, and on both sides of the chambers.

Australians generally have no absorbing concern about an agreement between two separate parties distinguished on the basis of race two centuries after the first wave of non-Aboriginal migration. But they may be open to negotiating and guaranteeing the place of Aborigines in the Commonwealth in a review and overhaul of the constitution leading up to its first centenary on 1 January 2001.

The task now at hand is to make a fresh assessment of the idea of an instrument of reconciliation, and to set down the non-negotiable parameters within which the process can proceed, hopefully with support from all major political parties and with community understanding. Then, Aborigines could belong again; this time in the society built on the land from which many of their ancestors were forever dispossessed.

On 12 June 1988, Aborigines in the Northern Territory issued the Barunga Statement, which set out their demands for land rights, compensation and a treaty. Mr Hawke joined his then Minister for Aboriginal Affairs in signing an agreement to negotiate a treaty with two Aboriginal elders representing the major land councils in the Northern Territory. The elder from the Centre, Wenten Rubuntja, spoke for his mob and explained the significance of the Barunga Statement in the Land Councils' *Land Rights News*:

Today there are lots of people living in this country. People who have come from all over the world. But we don't call them foreigners. We don't ask 'Where's your country? Where's your father from?' They have been born here. Their mothers' blood is in this country ... This is their country too now.

So all of us have to live together. We have to look after each other. We have to share this country. And this means respecting each other's laws and culture.

We have to work out a way of sharing this country, but there has to be an understanding of and respect of our culture, our law. Hopefully that's what this treaty will mean.[9]

I hope this book can be a non-Aboriginal contribution to sharing the country.

ONE:
THE UNRESOLVED ISSUES

The celebration of the bicentenary of the first fleet's landing at Sydney Cove was marked by national confusion about the place of Aborigines in Australia. The debate focussed on sovereignty, land rights, state rights, self-determination, compensation and talk of a treaty. One group of Aboriginal leaders claimed that their ancestors had never surrendered their right to undisturbed occupancy of their traditional lands; nor had they surrendered their political control over people entering their land. It was time for the new occupants to 'pay the rent'. Claiming that every square inch of the Australian landmass was under the control of some Aboriginal group before the invasion of the British, these leaders have argued that by 1788 there was an emerging Aboriginal national identity, if not an Aboriginal nation, which survives to this day. They have continued to argue that Aborigines have never surrendered their sovereignty. Another group of Aboriginal leaders were satisfied with being Australian citizens, but were concerned that Australian laws and policies be improved to give Aborigines a better deal, guaranteeing their control of their own affairs. Knowing there had to be compromise, they wanted equal bargaining power in negotiations with government. For them, autonomy within the Australian nation rather than sovereign separation was the issue. For the first group, a treaty would mean an agreement negotiated between separate nations governed by international law. For the other group, it would be a domestic agreement under

Australian law honoured by the parliaments and, if need be, enforced by the Australian courts.

In the end, the call for sovereignty may be no more than an ambit claim for more autonomy within the Australian nation. Some Aboriginal advocates continue to assert sovereignty in the strict sense. Their claims are not trans-latable simply into programmes and legal arrangements guaranteeing Aboriginal groups more autonomy in the life of the nation. For them, sovereignty is the major stumbling block to any proposals promoted by any political party in Australia. However, sovereignty in the strict sense is not and cannot be exercised by Aborigines as one distinct society in contemporary Australia. Debate about Aboriginal sovereignty can now be analysed only in terms of land rights and self-determination insofar as there is any achievable political outcome in contemporary Australia. This chapter analyses the issue of sovereignty and then outlines the gains that have been made in land rights in recent years and points to further gains that Aborigines can make. Then having dealt with the nature of contemporary federalism and the ongoing Australian concern with state rights, the chapter looks at how the idea of self-determination for indigenous people can be accommodated within a sovereign nation state constituted as a federation. The chapter concludes with a consideration of compen-sation and the proposal for many local treaties rather than one comprehensive national agreement.

Sovereignty

On 26 January 1788 an English sea captain, Arthur Phillip, came ashore with his party at Sydney Cove where they hoisted a flag, uttered a formula of words and set about running a penal institution. At that very moment, unbeknown to all concerned, Aborigines as far away as Arnhem Land became subjects of King George III. As ink spreads on blotting paper, so British sovereignty spread into the hinterland. Subsequent settlements at other geographic points served to consolidate British sovereignty over the whole continent. This sovereignty ensured that others (such as the French) were kept out and entailed the British Crown's assertion of control over the whole of the Australian mainland and Tasmania. It was not until 1879 that the Queensland Governor, on behalf of Queen Victoria, purported to annex the Torres Strait Islands thereby making Australia as we know it complete. In 1889 the Privy Council sanctioned all that had occurred, categorising the infant colony of New South Wales as 'a colony which consisted of a tract of territory practically unoccupied, without settled inhabitants or settled law, at the time when it was peacefully annexed to the British dominions'.[1] This legal fiction of *terra nullius* became firmly embedded in our history. Though a fiction, it has taken on a reality of its own that cannot be undone. But it continues to work an injustice upon the Aboriginal citizens of this nation and some of that injustice can be undone.

In 1978 Paul Coe, an Aboriginal barrister from Sydney, instituted proceedings in the High Court of Australia against the Commonwealth and the Government of the United Kingdom of Great Britain and Northern Ireland, seeking recognition of Aboriginal sovereignty over Australia. In his statement of claim to the court Coe asserted that he had authority from 'the whole aboriginal community and nation to bring this action'.[2] Sovereignty is that power in a State to which none other is superior; the supreme authority in an independent political society. In instituting these proceedings Coe was challenging the proposal that the Crown had effectively asserted sovereignty over the territory and people of Australia in 1788. He was attacking the presumption that Australia was *terra nullius* at that time, able to be claimed by any European power by settlement, rather than by cession resulting from a verifiable agreement with the natives or by conquest. Coe argued that there had been no effective transfer of sovereignty from the Aboriginal nation to the British Crown.

Coe was aided in his argument by the advisory opinion of the International Court of Justice (ICJ) in the *Western Sahara Case* decided in 1975. The ICJ hears cases between nation states and can also hear cases referred to it by the United Nations. In this case, there was a dispute between Morocco and the Mauritanian entity about sovereignty over the Western Sahara. At the time of Spanish colonisation, the tribes living in the Western Sahara had some ties of allegiance with the Sultan of Morocco. There were also legal ties between the Mauritanian entity and the territory of the Western Sahara. Morocco had claimed sovereignty over the Western Sahara on the basis of immemorial possession that had been allegedly uninterrupted and uncontested for centuries. Morocco had been the only independent State that existed in that region for a long period of time. Pointing to its geographical proximity to the territory and the territory's desert character, Morocco based its claim to title on 'continued display of authority'.[3] The court, assessing the evidence over the centuries, found that Morocco did not display effective and exclusive State activity in Western Sahara. There was simply a tie of allegiance between the Sultan and some, but only some, of the nomadic peoples of the territory.[4] This did not warrant international recognition of the Sultan's territorial sovereignty.[5] In the end, the ICJ could 'not establish any tie of territorial sovereignty between the territory of Western Sahara and the Kingdom of Morocco or the Mauritanian entity'.[6]

Presumably Coe was relying on the Western Sahara case to establish that the existence of legal ties between a sovereign state and some tribes in a territory does not of itself establish that state's sovereignty over the territory. Initially his case was heard in the High Court by Justice Mason (now the Chief Justice of Australia) who said that the Crown's sovereignty is unchallengeable in an Australian court. It would be impossible for a municipal court to entertain such an action because it was inconsistent with the accepted legal foundations of Australia that derived from British occupation and settlement and the exercise of legitimate authority. Also Justice Mason held that the Western Sahara case had no relevance to the domestic or municipal law of Australia.[7] The only circumstance in which the ICJ could conceivably be asked to adjudicate on Australian sovereignty would be if there were a dispute over Australian territory between sovereign states that are members of the UN. There is no way that Aborigines will ever be able to ask the International Court to adjudicate or advise on the British assertion of sovereignty over Australian territory and peoples in 1788.

Having failed to get to first base with Justice Mason, Coe gained no consolation by appealing to a full bench of the High Court. Justice Gibbs (with whom Justice Aickin concurred) held that the annexation of the east coast of Australia by Captain Cook in 1770 and the later acts by which the whole of the Australian continent became part of the dominions of the Crown, were acts of state whose validity could not be challenged.[8]

Gibbs distinguished Aboriginal tribes from those in the United States, which were seen as domestic nations. In his view, it was not possible to say that Australian Aborigines were organised as 'a distinct political society separated from others' or that they had ever been uniformly treated as a state. He found Coe's contentions impossible to maintain, asserting that 'there is no aboriginal nation, if by that expression is meant a people organised as a separate State or exercising any degree of sovereignty'.

Justice Jacobs concurred that the sovereignty issue could not be raised and resolved in a court exercising jurisdiction under the sovereignty that was being challenged.[9] No member of the bench was prepared to entertain a challenge to Australian sovereignty.

Coe's valiant attempt established that Aboriginal

sovereignty is not a matter that can be successfully challenged in Australian courts. Neither will it ever be adjudicated by the ICJ. Aboriginal sovereignty is at best a political claim. By asserting the continuation of their sovereignty, Aborigines are presumably seeking a legal basis on which to exercise power over land and resources and increased control of their own lives as individuals and communities. That basis will not emerge from any court declaration of sovereignty. It may result from some parliamentary acknowledgement of Aboriginal entitlements backed by a legal machinery for recognition and enforcement. Even that acknowledgement would make no reference to sovereignty. However, not all is lost.

Land Rights

Though Aborigines might have no legally recognisable claim to ongoing sovereignty, they may still have claims to land, which are enforceable in the courts. It is now academic whether British settlement in 1788 brought about a change of sovereignty or the assertion of sovereignty where none was previously recognisable. Neither situation meant the sovereign then owned all land in the new territory. Land ownership had to be determined by the domestic law of the territory. The British common law would not automatically displace an established system of law. If there were a vacuum of recognisable law, the common law would fill the gap upon the assertion of British sovereignty. But even if there were such a gap to European eyes, the common law, then being the domestic law of the territory, did not render all native inhabitants on their traditional lands as trespassers. They were lawful inhabitants, entitled to the protection of the common law.

A distinction is usually drawn between colonies acquired by conquest or cession and those acquired by settlement. The former are territories that had a system of law recognisable through European legal spectacles. The latter are territories that according to Justice Gibbs of the High Court 'had no civilised inhabitants or settled law'.

According to Gibbs, Australia has always been regarded as belonging to the latter class. The issue is not whether or not there were people living in the territory, but whether or not the people living in the territory had a system of law and social organisation sufficiently and immediately comprehensible to the European mindset at that time to permit negotiated agreement and accommodation of the native legal system.

In the Western Sahara case, the International Court of Justice looked at State practice in the international community in the latter part of the nineteenth century. Where territory was inhabited by tribes with their own social and political organisation, sovereignty was acquired by agreement with the tribal rulers. This transfer of sovereignty then provided the basis for the acquisition of title to land by the new sovereign. But the transfer of sovereignty did not automatically transfer title to any land over which the old inhabitants asserted control by virtue of continued occupancy.[10]

In Australia, there were no agreements with local rulers, and the British Crown obtained original title not through agreement but by occupation. Aboriginal legal systems were beyond the comprehension of the first British settlers. Cook and then Phillip had no idea even of the size of the Australian landmass, nor of its population. They did not encounter a social structure nor a broadly based resistance that easily allowed or required them to negotiate the terms of their settlement or occupation.

Upon the British settlement of the Australian colonies, the Crown assumed ultimate dominion over all lands. Systems of Aboriginal land law were not recognised; they were not even known to exist. Aboriginal land was not to be alienated to settlers without the consent of the Aboriginal traditional owners and in the colony of South Australia, in particular, the Colonial Office made special provision to protect Aboriginal land holdings. Any restrictions on land acquisition or transfer were self-imposed by the Crown. Even when colonial governments had been set up, the Colonial Office had retained the power to dispose of waste lands, allocating the revenue from sales to the maintenance of Her Majesty's public servants in the colonies. When responsible government was granted to the colonies, administration of Crown waste lands was transferred to the colonial governments.

At the frontier of pastoral expansion, the old and the new owners of the land engaged in bloody confrontations. The law of the new society extinguished the interest of the old and granted title to the new. At the frontier, Aborigines, being legally dispossessed, came to be trespassers in their own land. And so it was for seven generations.

In 1969 Aborigines at Yirrkala, disturbed by Nabalco's proposal to mine bauxite on their traditional lands, instituted proceedings in the Supreme Court of the Northern Territory claiming ownership of those lands. The court found against the Aborigines. In his decision Justice Blackburn asserted that he was 'not satisfied, on the balance of probabilities, that the plaintiffs' predecessors had in 1788 the same links to the same areas of land as those which the plaintiffs now claim'.[11] Even if they could have established their traditional links with the land, the plaintiffs would still have lost because the judge went on to decide that the traditional rights and interests of the Aborigines were not capable of recognition by the common law as property or, alternatively, that no Aboriginal rights or interests in land had survived the Crown's acquisition of the radical title to the land.[12]

Justice Blackburn was assisted in his decision by the judgment of a Canadian judge, which he regarded as weighty authority for two propositions:

1 In a settled colony there is no principle of communal native title except such as can be shown by prerogative

or legislative act, or a course of dealing.

2 In a settled colony a legislative and executive policy of treating the land of the colony as open to grant by the Crown, together with the establishment of native reserves, operates as an extinguishment of aboriginal title, if that ever existed.[13]

The Canadian judge's decision went on appeal all the way to the Supreme Court of Canada. When overruling the Canadian lower court decision, Justice Hall of the Supreme Court (with whom two other judges concurred) said Blackburn was wrong to accept the proposition that after conquest or discovery the native peoples have no rights at all except those subsequently granted or recognised by the conqueror or discoverer.[14]

In Australia, Blackburn's judgment was never made the subject of appeal. It was not until 1991 when the *Mabo* v *Queensland* case came to court that the High Court of Australia was given the opportunity to scrutinise Blackburn's judgment. The High Court has reserved its decision on Mabo's case, which relates to land title in the Torres Strait Islands. However, in 1979 Justice Gibbs (with whom Justice Aickin agreed) did say that its correctness was arguable;[15] Justice Murphy pointed out that the decision was 'not binding on this court';[16] and Justice Jacobs pointed out that there was no actual decision of the High Court that had determined that the Australian colonies were settled colonies.[17]

Even at the height of the colonial era, there was no doctrine that the colonising sovereign automatically took over unencumbered title to all land in the territory. Existing personal property rights continued until they were extinguished or otherwise dealt with by recognised action of the sovereign. Nor was there any doctrine that the sovereign would recognise only those forms of title that existed in the sovereign's own legal system. Those in actual occupation of land were presumed to have legal possession.[18] The presumption could of course be rebutted but only on the evidence of the particular case. New settlers could not gain title but from the Crown. Even if the Crown treated the territory as *terra nullius*, it could not treat occupied lands in the territory as vacant lands.

The real issue in the Australian context is whether or not the various Acts asserting sovereignty also entailed (expressly or by implication) the seizing of all lands, even those occupied since time immemorial by identifiable land-holding groups. If not seized by Act of State before or at the time of annexation, the lands could not be acquired later by the Crown except according to law. The sovereign's own law demands that there be a valid act of acquisition. This is a matter, unlike sovereignty, that can be reviewed by the domestic courts of the country.

Throughout the eighteenth century the European colonising powers in the international forum generally accepted that privately owned property was unaffected by the transfer of sovereignty until the new sovereign altered its status through its municipal law. Where property was communally owned and occupied, the practice was to reserve that land for the use of the native inhabitants. This applied particularly to large areas used for hunting and gathering purposes.[19]

So in Australia Aboriginal use and occupation of land that was communal and exclusive was not recognised as individual land title by the newly imported system of municipal law. Nevertheless it was still an interest in land capable of recognition and protection by the Crown. Lands that were not needed for economic development, particularly the traditional lands of remote communities, were set aside as reserves for Aboriginal purposes and remained under the control of the Crown. It was common for such lands to be vested in a Crown official as trustee for the Aboriginal community.

Even when the Crown had not created a formal trust, Crown officials had a duty to retain and protect reserve lands for local Aborigines who had been forcibly moved there to make way for pastoral expansion or to avoid further mixing of the races. Many vulnerable Aborigines have had their interest in those lands affected adversely by Crown officials paying insufficient regard to their duty to protect the Aborigines.

The vast pastoral leases that were granted to new settlers usually contained provision for continued Aboriginal use and occupation for hunting and gathering purposes. Aborigines were still free to inhabit lands that had not been alienated to new settlers. Legal dispossession was not effected in an instant at the proclamation of British sovereignty. Rather it continued over two centuries each time a new law or Order in Council was added to the thicket of Australian land laws allowing new settlers to encroach further on to Aboriginal land, usually without compensation or consent.

In the past fifteen years most Australian governments have pursued a policy of instituting local Aboriginal control and ownership of these reserve lands under a statutory title. Whereas previously the areas of these reserves could be reduced at will by the government of the day without legislative warrant, court process or compensation, the vesting of title and control has secured these lands for future generations of Aboriginal people. Obviously this can be done without cost to any other citizens. With adaptation, it extends the protection of our system of law to Aboriginal communities as the owners of their lands. These arrangements have been aimed at rectifying some of the injustices brought about by our common law inherited from Britain, based on the simplistic legal fiction that the whole of Australia was unoccupied and ungoverned in 1787. In the Yirrkala case the court found that each group did have its own law, which was described as:

a subtle and elaborate system highly adapted to the country in which people lived their lives, which provided a stable order of society and was remarkably free from the vagaries of personal whim or influence ... 'a government of laws, and not of men'.[20]

In 1982 a group of Torres Strait Islanders representing the traditional owners of three islands, initiated proceedings in the High Court of Australia. They claimed that the islands had been continuously inhabited and exclusively possessed by their people, who lived in permanent settled communities with their own social and political organisation. They claimed that the annexation of their islands by the Governor of Queensland and the Queensland Coast Islands Act of the Queensland Parliament in 1879, though extending the sovereignty of Queen Victoria to the islands, did so subject to the continued enjoyment of their rights until those rights had been extinguished by the sovereign. Further they claimed that their rights had not been extinguished, which would mean that their continued rights were recognised by the Australian municipal system of law.

In April 1985 the Queensland Parliament passed the Queensland Coast Islands Declaratory Act, innocuously described as an Act 'to allay doubts that may exist concerning certain islands forming part of Queensland'. The Act declared that 'upon the islands being annexed' in 1879, 'the islands were vested in the Crown in right of Queensland freed from all other rights, interests and claims of any kind whatsoever'. It provided that:

No compensation was or is payable to any person in respect of any right, interest or claim alleged to have existed prior to the annexation of the islands ... or in respect of any right, interest or claim alleged to derive from such a right, interest or claim.[21]

Introducing the legislation, the Deputy Premier said:

The passage of this Bill will, it is hoped, remove the necessity for limitless research work being undertaken in relation to the position of the relevant Torres Strait Islands prior to annexation and will prevent interminable argument in the Courts on matters of history.[22]

Doubts and argument were to be resolved by retro-spectively extinguishing rights that (arguably) still existed, and this without payment of compensation. 'Interminable argument on matters of history' may be a waste of time unless, as in this case, those matters of history affect the present claims of citizens that still await adjudication in the courts. This Act of 1985 (not 1788 or 1879) contributed nothing to the resolution of the injustice, described by Justice Deane of the High Court in a judgment delivered one month before the Queensland Government introduced this legislation to Parliament:

The almost two centuries that have elapsed since white settlement have seen the extinction of some Aboriginal clans and the dispersal, with consequent loss of identity and tradition, of others. Particularly where the clan has survived as a unit living on ancestral lands, however, the relationship between the Aboriginal peoples and their land remains unobliterated. Yet, almost two centuries on, the generally accepted view remains that the common law is ignorant of any communal native title or other legal claim of the Aboriginal clans or peoples even to ancestral tribal lands on which they still live. If that view of the law be correct, and I do not suggest that it is not, the common law of this land has still not reached the stage of retreat from injustice which the law of Illinois and Virginia had reached in 1823 when Marshall CJ accepted that, subject to the assertion of ultimate dominion by the State, the 'original inhabitants' should be recognised as having 'a legal as well as just claim' to retain the occupancy of their traditional lands.[23]

The Queensland Coast Islands Declaratory Act was challenged in the High Court of Australia by Mr Eddie Mabo and other residents of Murray Island. It was found to be contrary to the Racial Discrimination Act, which had been enacted by the Commonwealth Parliament to implement the International Convention on the Elimination of All Forms of Discrimination. Three judges of the High Court described the 'draconian' effect of the Queensland law 'to extinguish the rights which the plaintiffs claim in their traditional homeland and to deny the right to compensation in respect of that extinction'.[24] Another judge, confining the scope of the Queensland law, referred to 'long established notions of justice that can be traced back at least to the guarantee of Magna Carta against the arbitrary disseisin [taking away] of freehold'.[26] The High Court is yet to determine whether the residents of Murray Island retained property rights after the Crown asserted sovereignty over their island. If their property rights survived until 1975, the Racial Discrimination Act would now frustrate any attempt by the Queensland Parliament to extinguish only those rights.[26]

The blanket application to the Australian continent of the British common law and eighteenth century European international law has not obliterated the moral claim of Aborigines to the continued use and enjoyment of their lands. It is still to be determined by the High Court whether the common law recognises any ongoing Aboriginal interest in land. If recognised, that interest would be a legal encumbrance to Crown title, which requires that the protection of the common law be extended to Aborigines and their interests in their traditional lands. Many Aborigines still have a moral claim to identifiable areas of land 200 years later, a claim that may be legally recognised and able to be protected under legislation such as the Racial Discrimination Act.

Where a community has continued to live on its traditional land, discharging its spiritual obligations with regard to that land, and that land has never been occupied by any other persons, that community is morally entitled to a legal title. To deny legal title to that land would be to complete the act of dispossession commenced over 200 years ago, or else it would be to deny the operation of the rule of law with respect to these citizens and their most precious possession.

Where a community has been moved from its traditional land and no other people have a moral claim to the original land, the community should be granted title in restitution. Where an Aboriginal community consists of people who have been moved from their traditional lands to make way for pastoral or other development and there is now no question of restoring their traditional land to them because other people have subsequently gained their own moral claims to it through occupancy, labour and expenditure, the community is entitled to compensation. If that community has been moved from its traditional land but has remained an identifiable group on identifiable land to which no other persons have title, the community is entitled to title as compensation for what they lost.

Aborigines living in or about urban areas are no longer living on large areas of identifiable Aboriginal land. They no longer live together as traditional communities. And yet they are the ones who have suffered most through dispossession. The forebears of these urban- or fringe-dwellers are from various groups and often from other races. They identify themselves as Aborigines, having an Aboriginal ancestry, and being accepted as members of the local Aboriginal community. Generally, for them, the land rights initiatives of recent years have done little. Their traditional lands can no longer be restored to them.

For urban Aborigines, there is little suitable land and often no identifiable group with the same ancestry for there to be a communal land grant in compensation. Rather what they seek is assistance with their great needs, including land for residence and business, and the transition to an urban existence. Our society is less than welcoming to those for whom dispossession has meant often not only loss of culture but also loss of family and there is a yearning to belong and a desire to exercise power for the benefit of self and community. It has been the dispossession of these Australians on which we have constructed the monolith that is Australian society and its prosperity. This is not to argue that we must pay reparation for the sins of our forebears perpetrated on others' forebears. It is to say that we have a duty to share the fruits of those sins with those who suffered by them and who continue to suffer. We must compensate them for their loss.

Of course, these principles of justice would have to be qualified if land, the resource in question, were scarce and if the exercise of collective power by the group were to interfere unduly with the individual's entitlement to choose between a more traditional Aboriginal lifestyle and that of other Australians. The application of the principles need not result in any citizens losing their house, beach house, farm or even their vacant block. Aboriginal rights and claims to land are usually restricted to unalienated Crown lands.

Society has a responsibility not only to recognise the land rights of remote Aboriginal communities but also to fulfil the land needs and to accommodate the legitimate aspirations of urban and fringe-dwelling Aborigines. Concern for the plight of the poor, dispossessed, and powerless non-Aboriginal person does not excuse us from considering that of the Aborigine, whose claim against the state is stronger because in almost every instance it was the state that compounded the Aborigine's plight by discriminatory laws and policies over seven generations.

Most remaining Aboriginal reserve land throughout Australia has now been handed over to local Aboriginal ownership and control, though there was very little reserve land remaining in the eastern states south of Cape York. Nineteen per cent of the Northern Territory remained Aboriginal reserve and has now been transferred to land trusts composed of traditional owners. These lands are inalienable in that they cannot be sold off or resumed by the Northern Territory Parliament. Eighteen per cent of South Australia is included in the Pitjantjatjara and

Maralinga land titles. Eight per cent of Western Australia is Aboriginal reserve land that is now to be leased to local communities for a ninety-nine year term. Two per cent of Queensland is reserve that is now being granted to local councils as trustees for their communities.

In the Northern Territory, Aborigines may make traditional land claims to unalienated Crown land outside towns provided the land is not set aside for a public purpose. To succeed, the claimants must establish affiliations that place them under a primary spiritual responsibility for the sites and the land. Thirteen per cent of the Territory has been successfully claimed and claims over another 13 per cent await determination. If all claims are successful, 45 per cent of the Northern Territory will eventually be classed as Aboriginal land.

In New South Wales, Aborigines have been able to make claims to vacant Crown land not required for public purposes, though little such land exists. Of the land tax collected from 1984 until 1999, 7.5 per cent (presently $14 million per annum) is being allocated to NSW land councils for land purchases and running expenses. The Greiner Government has moved to make this money more available for general welfare and delivery of government services. In Queensland, Aborigines can claim vacant Crown land outside towns and cities once the land is gazetted as available for claim.

Especially in Northern Australia, there are still traditional Aboriginal owners of land who have common 'affiliations that place the group under a primary spiritual responsibility' for the sites and land.[27] There can be no doubting that for these people 'the fundamental truth about the Aboriginals' relationship to the land is that whatever else it is, it is a religious relationship'.[28] Before becoming a judge, Justice Brennan was counsel for the Northern Land Council in the Woodward Royal Commission on Aboriginal Land Rights. In this role he was one of the original architects of the Land Rights Act.[29] On the High Court, he has drawn a distinction between the owners of land under Anglo–Australian law who are vested with a bundle of rights exercisable with respect to land, and traditional Aboriginal owners whose only right under the Land Rights Act is the right to forage, without excluding others. The relationship between the people and the land is not defined by rights, but by the 'group's spiritual affiliations to a site on the land and the group's spiritual responsibility for the site and for the land. Aboriginal ownership is primarily a spiritual affair rather than a bundle of rights'.[30]

Paul Seaman QC, who conducted the ill-fated Aboriginal Land Inquiry in Western Australia, found that although 'the great majority of people of Aboriginal descent in Western Australia can make the case that they or their forebears were forcibly dispossessed of traditional lands, many would be unable to obtain any land under a process which demanded proof of Aboriginal tradition'.[31]

There is now a whole spectrum of Aboriginal relationships to land, from the communal, traditional and religious, to the individual and economic. Bases for claim and forms of title must vary accordingly. There has not been any treaty, compact, or constitutional guarantee for the preservation of Aboriginal community lands. It is necessary for the law of the land to accord whatever legal security it can for such lands. A communal title for the benefit of a group whose membership changes over time requires a constant legal entity in which to vest the title – a corporation or a trustee. Community members then need to be assured that the trustees (even though they may include their own members) cannot sell the land, give it away or create long-term interests in the land without their consent or without their communal interests being considered. In order to ensure maximum security of tenure the government of the day should not be permitted to re-acquire the land compulsorily unless that be the specific will of the Parliament.

Aboriginal communities want the best form of title that

our law can give (namely freehold), except that they usually require that their heritage and that of their children not be capable of alienation against their communal interest. In shorthand, this form of title has been called inalienable freehold. Though inalienability is the cherished desire of many Aboriginal communities, there are some communities who are now anxious to utilise some of their lands as capital assets or for economic purposes, for community or even individual enterprises. Land rights legislation usually places strict limits not only on the power of sale and surrender but also on the power to mortgage and lease.

All landowners have the right to exclude trespassers from their land. Every week, holders of vast pastoral leases place advertisements in country newspapers stating: 'Any person found shooting or otherwise trespassing on X station will be prosecuted. Any previous permission cancelled from this date'. This right is exercisable by remote Aboriginal communities also. A problem arises with a communal landholder in that there is a need for a legal entity or collection of persons with the power to give permission on behalf of the group. For a remote Aboriginal community, there is the further problem of communication of request and acceptance. So in South Australia it is the land-holding corporation, through its officers, that is empowered to grant or refuse permission. In the Northern Territory the task has been given to land councils, which are required by law to consult with the traditional owners before granting or refusing permission.

Most land rights legislation contains special penalties for unauthorised entry on Aboriginal land. It is perverse to argue that a permit system is apartheid. As Justice Brennan of the High Court has said: 'The difference between land rights and apartheid is the difference between a home and a prison.'[32] Through legal protection of an Aboriginal community's land rights, Aborigines are assured the right to choose between their traditional lifestyle on their land and life elsewhere. Outsiders are allowed access to Aboriginal land only with the consent of the landowners. Unlike the Northern Territory and South Australia, Queensland has modified the permit system so that the town areas of community lands are viewed as public areas for which permission of access is not required, while council permission is necessary to enter other community lands. Councils have power to punish infringements under their by-laws.

In Queensland, Victoria and Tasmania, Aborigines have no legal right to hunt and gather on pastoral leases. In South Australia such rights are reserved under most leases. In Western Australia, Aborigines have access to unimproved, unenclosed pastoral lands. In the Northern Territory, Aboriginal access is confined to those having a traditional relationship to the land. The Torres Strait Treaty recognises the traditional fishing rights of the islanders. Fishing adjacent to Aboriginal land is generally permitted without need for licences and Aboriginal communities are given no special protection from commercial fishing that may disrupt their traditional life. In the Northern Territory, traditional owners can apply for sea closures and some communities have been granted community fishing licences.

Last century it was the pastoralists who were primarily responsible for overriding Aboriginal interests in land. In recent years the conflict of claims has arisen between miners and Aborigines. Under our law, minerals are generally owned by the Crown, not the landholder, and the vast underpopulated and undeveloped areas of land in Australia are generally open to mining activity without the need for the land-holder's consent.

In some States there are still non-Aboriginal landowners who own the minerals in their land, title having been granted last century when there was no notion that the Crown retained ownership of all sub-surface minerals. In New South Wales, Aboriginal owners have the right to minerals except gold, silver, coal and petroleum. In all other jurisdictions, the minerals on Aboriginal land belong to the Crown.

On non-Aboriginal land, mining usually cannot occur on private, improved land without the permission of the landholder, nor can it occur without consent on small suburban blocks even if they are unimproved. Improved land includes gardens, orchards, recreation grounds, burial places and places of worship. To mine on other unimproved private lands the miner must have a permit from the mining warden, which can be issued without the consent of the landholder. In Western Australia farmers still have an unrestricted power to veto exploration or mining on their cultivated land; this power cannot be over-ridden by government, even in the national interest.

In the Northern Territory, the original 1976 land rights legislation provided that an exploration permit or mining interest on Aboriginal land could be granted only with the consent of the traditional owners. This right of veto was limited and had been advocated by every commission of inquiry that investigated the matter since 1972. The consent of traditional owners was never required for a mining interest that was in substantial accordance with proposals considered at the time Aboriginal consent was given to exploration. Neither was consent required for projects for which permits had been issued before June 1976. The Governor General always retained the power to override traditional owners' withholding of consent in the national interest.

Before the 1987 dissolution of Parliament, the Hawke Government legislated to restrict further Aboriginal control of mining on their lands in the Northern Territory. Aborigines still have a power of veto (subject to the national interest) in the sense that they are able to say 'no' to exploration and mining. However if they express interest in exploration, they are not able to withdraw their consent from mining. They have a year to negotiate terms and conditions, and in the absence of agreement, these matters are determined by an arbitrator. This new scheme reduces the 'say' that traditional owners have over mining activity on their land; it also reduces their bargaining power with mining companies. The scheme favours the miners more than any proposed by any of the independent judicial inquiries into the vexed question. It happens to reflect substantially the wishes of the mining industry whose views were specifically rejected by Justice Toohey in 1983.

In New South Wales, Aboriginal landowners exercise a general control over mining on their land. In Victoria, the landholding corporations of Lake Condah and Framlingham Forest may withhold consent to exploration or mining but their refusal may be overturned by an arbitrator. In Queensland if the community council refuses to give consent to a mining lease, the State government may still approve the lease having taken into account the views of the relevant community council. In South Australia, there is provision for a tribunal to arbitrate disputes when consent is refused or the terms and conditions for consent are unresolved. The arbitrator's determination is binding on all parties, including the Crown.

In the Northern Territory, royalty equivalents are paid into an Aboriginals Benefit Trust Account (ABTA), which are distributed under the direction of the Commonwealth Minister for Aboriginal Affairs to the Northern, Central and Tiwi Land councils. The ABTA Advisory Committee invests 50 per cent of income for the establishment of a capital base. Traditional owners receive payments from the land councils for mining occurring on their land. Since March 1983, royalty equivalents of more than $40 million have been paid into the ABTA. In South Australia, one-third of any royalty payment goes to the corporation of local Aboriginal owners, one-third for the benefit of Aborigines generally and one-third to the State. In New South Wales, all royalties from mining, if any, go to the tiered land councils. In Victoria, any royalties from mining on the Lake Condah or Framlingham Forest lands would be paid into Aboriginal trust funds. In Queensland, Aboriginal and Torres Strait Islander communities used to enjoy a 3 per cent share in profits from mining on their land. This entitlement does not apply to any mining projects commenced after 1984, but they receive a share in royalties determined by government.

Any Aborigine can apply to the Commonwealth Minister for Aboriginal Affairs for a declaration that a significant Aboriginal area, even though on private land, be protected from damage or desecration. If State laws are inadequate to provide protection that is warranted, the minister may make a declaration that results in interference with the area being an offence. A declaration must be advertised and can be revoked by the minister or either House of Parliament. In an emergency, approved public servants can make a declaration that is valid for up to forty-eight hours. If a declaration were to result in the acquisition of private land, the owner must be compensated by the Commonwealth. A long-term declaration can be made only after the minister has considered the report of an independent expert who assesses the representations of interested parties. Declarations over sacred objects and Aboriginal human remains can also be sought. The States and the Northern Territory also have legislative arrangements for the protection of Aboriginal heritage. The Victorian Aboriginal Cultural Heritage is protected by a separate Commonwealth Act.

It is often alleged that Aborigines discover sacred sites after development activity has commenced. The essence of a very sacred site is that it is kept secret from all but initiated members. It was a mining company, not Aborigines, that was exposed in the High Court for not specifying the precise location of a precious mineral deposit. As Justice Mason put it: 'One reason given was the commercial sensitivity of that information, but a further explanation may well be that the imprecision ... supported a submission made by (the company) ... that the whole of the block be excised from any land recommended for grant' to the traditional owners.[33]

Land rights legislation in all its variety is here to stay. This legislative mosaic is a belated attempt by the parliaments of the nation to set right injustices in the simple cases, chiefly where there are still identifiable communities with access to ancestral lands in which no other citizens have an interest. There have been attempts by the Commonwealth to speed up this process and to complement actions of the states, but inevitably they stop short at the barrier of state rights.

State Rights

Before 1967 the Commonwealth constitution had provided that Aborigines were not to be counted in the official population of Australia. Neither did the Commonwealth Parliament have the power to make laws for Aborigines. In 1965 the Menzies Government had considered putting a referendum to the people to delete the enigmatic directive in the constitution that Aborigines were not to be counted, but it did not favour a proposal to give the Commonwealth power to legislate for Aborigines. Menzies thought this could have 'most undesirable results', leading to the institution of 'industrial, social, criminal and other laws relating exclusively to Aborigines'.[34] Although that view still has its adherents to this day, it was rejected by the Holt Government, which eventually moved a referendum proposal to give the Commonwealth Parliament concurrent legislative power with the States concerning Aborigines.[35] The proposal was supported by all major political parties. The Parliament stated that the purpose of the amendment was:

to make it possible for the Commonwealth Parliament to make special laws for the people of the Aboriginal race, wherever they may live, if the Commonwealth Parliament considers this desirable or necessary ... This would not mean that the States would automatically lose their existing powers. What is intended is that the National Parliament could make laws, if it thought fit, relating to Aboriginals – as it can about many other matters on which the States also have the power to legislate. The Commonwealth's object will be to co-operate with the States to ensure that together we act in the best interests of the Aboriginal people of Australia.[36]

The referendum was carried overwhelmingly, with five million voting in favour and only half a million against.

So before 1967 the States had the exclusive power to make laws for Aborigines within their territory. After 1967 both the Commonwealth and the States had the power, which could be exercised concurrently, but in the case of any inconsistency the exercise of Commonwealth power would prevail. The 1967 referendum brought about a new distribution of legislative and policy making power concerning Aborigines. Advocates for 'States rights' have continued to argue that State governments should have the final say on Aboriginal affairs. However, State rights is a political slogan and has no place in the correct determination of the distribution of legislative power. In this context States, like the Commonwealth, do not have rights. Only people have rights. States, like the Commonwealth, have power to make laws and to implement policies. Two justices of the High Court have indicated that the circumstances of the 1967 referendum created not only a Commonwealth power but also a responsibility towards Aborigines – a national responsibility to the descendants of the nation's first and dispossessed inhabitants. In the Franklin Dam case, which saved the Tasmanian wilderness, Justice Brennan said the 1967 amendment of the constitution was 'an affirmation of the will of the Australian people that the odious policies of oppression and neglect of Aboriginal citizens were to be at an end'.[37] Justice Deane suggested that it had made clear that there was a need for acceptable laws and policies 'to mitigate the effects of past barbarism'.[38] The Commonwealth's power to make laws for Aborigines provided, in part, a constitutional basis for the Commonwealth to override action by the Tasmanian Government that would have threatened the environment and Aboriginal sites of significance.

Obviously land rights legislation is a matter of primary concern to the local State parliaments. But the Commonwealth has the power and responsibility to meet the needs and aspirations of Aborigines for land when State parliaments fail to act, as has been the case in Tasmania. The existence of this responsibility demands the exercise of Commonwealth power when these needs and aspirations remain unaddressed. The interests of Aborigines would be best served by federal–State co-operation; but if this is not forthcoming, the Commonwealth responsibility remains, as does the power. It is then a matter of political will and diplomacy in the delivery of land rights with community acceptance.

To exercise its constitutional power, the Commonwealth Parliament would have to compensate a State on just terms for any property that it acquired. There are significant doubts about what restrictions or benefits, in relation to land, amount to property for the purposes of compensation. For example, the Commonwealth can place some planning restrictions on land use without compensating the owner. If those restrictions were to render the land unusable, the owner would be entitled to compensation. The vesting of meaningful title to land in an Aboriginal community, in circumstances where a State has refused to vest that title, would amount to an acquisition of land. The unresolved question is: What are just terms between the Commonwealth and a State for the vesting of title in Aborigines for reserve land on which they have always lived or to which they have always had unrestricted access? As land reserved by States for Aborigines is occupied and dedicated to a particular purpose, just terms may well be significantly less than the market value of the vacant land. After all such land is supposed to remain dedicated to the use of Aborigines for as long as it is required.

Although it has the power to do so, the Commonwealth has never compulsorily acquired land in the States for Aborigines. The time may come when it is in the public interest that this power be exercised, but it is hard to conceive it being to the political advantage of any government. However, talk of State rights should not be used to avoid a Commonwealth responsibility. When a State fails to exercise the power, to the detriment of its citizens, the Commonwealth must assume the responsibility. Of course, there is no legal impediment to the Commonwealth providing funds for the purchase of land on the open market for the benefit of Aborigines.

Once Aborigines are assured an adequate land base, whether by State or Commonwealth action, it should be easier for the Commonwealth to pursue a policy of self-determination, encouraging Aboriginal communities to manage their own affairs. Hopefully this can be done in co-operation with State government departments that deliver services.

Self-Determination

After the 1967 referendum, the Commonwealth Government set up the Council for Aboriginal Affairs chaired by Dr H. C. Coombs. The other members were Barrie Dexter, who later became the first secretary of the Department of Aboriginal Affairs and the anthropologist, Professor W. E. H. Stanner. On Australia Day 1972, Prime Minister William McMahon set down a Commonwealth policy in Aboriginal Affairs that Stanner called the 'doctrine of four Aboriginal freedoms':

By this doctrine Aborigines are now entitled to decide for themselves, or at least to try to decide, four things which were not open to them in the past. First they may decide for themselves to what *degree* they will identify with what the Prime Minister called 'one Australian society'. Second, they may decide for themselves at what *rate* they will so identify. Thirdly, they have the right to *preserve* their own culture and fourth, the right to *develop* their own culture.[39]

The policy of assimilation was ditched, and Aborigines came onto the political agenda. For the first time at a federal level, all major political parties made commitments to Aboriginal welfare, advancement and even rights. Stanner thought that 1972 had some claim to being remembered as 'The Year of the Blackfellow'. He accurately predicted that 'Aboriginal affairs are . . . now in all probability irretrievably political'.[40]

Various buzzwords have been used since 1972: integration, self-management, self-sufficiency, and self-determination. They are terms of political art rather than legal precision. The more political Aboriginal leaders have made self-determination their clarion call, although this term is now unacceptable to the Liberal and National Parties at a federal level. However at a State level, the Greiner Government has been happy to use it in describing its amendments to the New South Wales Land Rights Act. The Hawke Government has been ambivalent about the use of the term. It does not see it as unacceptable but prefers the term 'self-management'. The Coalition adds the term 'self-sufficiency' to self-management so as to connote economic development rather than welfare dependency. Integration is a term of the past. Aborigines committed to self-determination see the possibility of constituting themselves as another order of government in the federal structure of Australia. To date, governments have been prepared to concede local government status to Aboriginal communities. Some Aborigines argue that just as they are permitted to perform their own local government functions, so too they should be able to perform in their communities some of the services and roles of State and Commonwealth government. They might then come to determine their future, not merely managing their present, in accordance with policy directives from State and Commonwealth governments.

In international law, self-determination has come to have a technical meaning in the decolonisation process. When a colonial power is withdrawing from a territory, the people of the territory are to be assured a free choice in determining their political future. By a 1960 resolution of the General Assembly, the UN made a 'Declaration on the Granting of Independence to Colonial Countries and Peoples' that proclaims the right of all peoples to determine freely their political status and pursue freely their economic, social and cultural development.[41] In recent years, indigenous representatives and their advocates have attempted to argue, by analogy that their people are 'peoples' in the international law sense who also have the collective right to determine their future, whether as part of the nation state in which they presently live, or even as a separate state or entity with international recognition. Governments, on the other hand, are only prepared to concede internal self-determination, which would entitle indigenous groups to more autonomy within the domestic political arrangements of the nation. They are not prepared to recognise external self-determination, which carries the right to separate nationhood and autonomous sovereignty.

There is now a domestic meaning of self-determination, which connotes more than self-management. It incorporates the notion that indigenous organisations and representatives should be able to shape policy for their people and not simply manage government programmes, run co-operative enterprises and administer local government functions for communities that happen to be indigenous. This is a political term rather than a legal definition. Continued attempts by Aboriginal leaders to extend it to self-determination in the international law sense take no account of the provision in the UN resolution, which states, that 'any attempt aimed at the partial or total disruption of the national unity and the territorial integrity of a country is incompatible with the purpose and principles of the Charter of the United Nations'.[42]

A racially or ethnically distinct group does not necessarily constitute a 'people' in international law. In the Western Sahara case the International Court found that the principle of self-determination had broadened since 1960 to include 'the need to pay regard to the freely expressed will of peoples'. But having reviewed various instances where the General Assembly had dispensed with the need for consultation with the inhabitants of a territory, the International Court found that there had been cases where the group did not constitute a 'people' entitled to self-determination or where consultation was unnecessary, presumably because the people had been absorbed for so long as part of the state or were not in a territorially separate area.[43]

Aborigines like Michael Mansell and Bob Weatherall who form the Aboriginal Provisional Government have expressed dissatisfaction with self-determination being confined to the domestic sense. They see it as little more than self-management, which permits Aborigines to manage programmes only after they have been determined by politicians and public servants. It leaves Aborigines at the end of the line as recipients of the system. Fred Chaney argued in 1989, as Leader of the Opposition in the Senate, that it was just another semantic issue:

One of the most common points of policy since ... the 1970s has been the view that, under one name or another, governments should be encouraging Aboriginal people to take control of their own lives. This is sometimes called self-management, sometimes self-determination.[44]

Politicians like Chaney have wanted to avoid the term

self-determination on the grounds that 'it can have political connotations which have nothing to do with the social advancement that we are concerned about'. He is happy to speak of Aboriginal independence as 'personal independence and community independence, not political independence'. Chaney's concern is that too much is expected of under-resourced, untrained, remote communities in the name of self-management and that it is a romantic ideal to hope that Aborigines will want to do everything for themselves.

Labor Governments since the Whitlam era have sometimes used the term self-determination, but usually confine themselves to self-management. In his formal ministerial statements to Parliament, Mr Hawke confines himself to self-management and 'full accountability for the expenditure of public funds'. As Minister for Aboriginal Affairs, Mr Hand was happy to speak also of 'the need for self-determination' so that our 'claims to being a civilised, mature and humane society' would not ring hollow.[45]

Just before the Department of Aboriginal Affairs went out of existence at the beginning of 1990, a senior departmental officer gave a frank assessment of Labor's approach:

The Whitlam and subsequent Labor governments put forth 'self-determination' as their central policy in Aboriginal affairs but seemed reluctant, or at least tardy, in giving effect and substance to the proper meaning of the policy by allowing Aboriginals to place their hands on the controls of the system.

Comparing the Coalition's 'self-management' policy, he accurately concluded:

In the end there was no difference in the two policies – they became confused and synonymous with each other with the stronger term being diminished to the meaning of the weaker.[46]

It may be that self-management and self-sufficiency are all

our politicians are prepared to offer. They are the terms used three times in the ATSIC legislation, which was the crowning achievement of Hand's ministry. The term self-determination does not appear in the Act. The weaker terms may even be the right terms to describe the modest aspirations of most Aborigines two centuries after self-determination was first denied. Some vocal and informed Aborigines definitely want more. Even if we do not subscribe to the separate nation idea, we must as a community remain open to allowing the descendants of the traditional owners of this land to determine their future as well as to manage their own affairs, to set their agenda, though subject to the constitution and laws of the Commonwealth.

Even communities now granted title to their community lands suffer irremediable interference from government with insufficient regard for the principles of self-management and self-determination. One recent example of this interference concerns the Yarrabah Aboriginal community land outside Cairns in North Queensland.

The largest single landholding to be affected by the World Heritage Listing of the Queensland Wet Tropical Rainforests was the Yarrabah community land. For a variety of reasons, none of which convinced the Minister for the Environment, Senator Richardson, the Yarrabah Council opposed the listing. The Commonwealth Government treated Yarrabah like any other private landholder. There was no consideration for principles of self-management and self-determination.

In June 1988 the International Union for Conservation of Nature and Natural Resources (IUCN) submitted its report on the proposed listing to the bureau of the World Heritage Committee in Paris. The IUCN said they still needed clarification of 'the position of the Aboriginal owners on the question of inclusion of their land' and that 'further consultation is essential and in progress'.[47]

The bureau requested that the Australian authorities

provide information on 'land ownership by Aboriginal peoples' by 1 October 1988. The international agencies were not happy at the idea of including Aboriginal land unless the owners were involved in and fully endorsed the aims of the convention in their area as at Uluru and Kakadu.

The chairman of the Yarrabah Council, Peter Noble, wrote to Senator Richardson on 28 June 1988, saying:

There is no way we could ever approve the inclusion of any of our land unless we were to receive satisfactory answers to our outstanding queries. Though the regulations will permit our continued traditional and community use of forestry resources, we would not be able to exploit commercially our forestry resources without your consent. You could grant such consent having regard 'only to the protection, conservation and presentation' of the area. Your consent could be subject to judicial review instigated by outside lobby groups.

This potential interference with our rights to self-management and self-determination could not receive our agreement if there were no tangible benefits to be received by the community. If there be no tangible benefits and such potential interference with our land rights, we would have no option but to continue strenuous opposition to our lands being included in the listing.

We do not want to be made the meat in the sandwich in an ongoing Federal–State conflict. We hope you can come to Yarrabah soon to discuss these matters.

Senator Richardson did not meet with the Yarrabah Council until 18 October, a fortnight after he had provided the Secretariat of the World Heritage Bureau with clarification of outstanding matters including, presumably, Aboriginal views on the listing. The council was not told what clarification, if any, had been provided. The Senator was then to respond by letter to points raised by the council within a fortnight of their meeting. No response was received until 23 November, the last scheduled meeting date for the Yarrabah Council to consider the matter before the World Heritage Committee's determination in Brasilia.

Aboriginal concern with outside interference with their land rights went unheeded. Senator Richardson said Yarrabah would be subjected to 'an overall management plan' and that the Government would be concerned if the council 'proposed to undertake activities involving wholesale clearance of areas of rainforest or other threats to World Heritage values'.

In his letter of 23 November 1988, Senator Richardson asked Yarrabah to provide 'plans or details of future logging and possible expansion of sawmill operations', and 'plans for outstation development'. The carrots for agreeing to such interference in their affairs were to be: a financial package to assist with 'private business initiatives which employ displaced workers', the Senator's desire 'to see a programme of Aboriginal ranger training', the possibility of 'employment opportunities for Aboriginals with the proposed Rainforest Authority', and other programmes that 'could also be examined' to 'identify additional employment opportunities for Aboriginals'.

Mr Noble replied next day:

Basically, you have offered us nothing but the assurance that we will still be able to use our land as we do presently, if all goes well. The cost to us will be the uncertainty and time involved in gaining approval from outside bodies for our land use including outstation development.

The only things you have offered us in return for the interference with our land rights and self-management are the ability to apply for funds which are 'for assistance with private business initiatives which employ displaced workers' and a possible programme of Aboriginal ranger training. As you know, we will not have any displaced workers because we are not presently engaged in commercial logging. We will have our own ranger programme in place early in 1989.

We have not wanted to be involved in the public political debate about World Heritage Listing. We thought you would do more to consult with us. We thought you would have more regard for our land rights and self-management. The IUCN said further consultation was 'essential and in progress'. Yet you have never been here. You did not reply to our letter of 28 June 1988. No one addressed our concerns expressed in our submission to the Rainforest Unit dated 7 July 1988. We finally met with you on 18 October 1988, only to find that our inclusion in World Heritage Listing was non-negotiable and that you had sent revised boundaries to the international committee on 1 October 1988.

You do not seem to understand that we as an Aboriginal community are sick of outside interference in our affairs. There is nothing in your proposal to help us. The interference in our local affairs will not be taken away by allowing one Aboriginal representative on the Consultative Committee.

Like our previous council, we oppose the listing of our land. If listed, it will be without our consent.

And so their lands were listed. Replying to public comment by Senator Richardson, Mr Noble wrote again on 5 February 1989 reiterating Yarrabah's opposition to the listing, claiming that government consultation was 'absolutely minimal' and 'firmly oriented towards convincing us of the error of our ways'. Senator Richardson made his first visit to Yarrabah on 8 August 1989. He and the council reached agreement on compensation and land management procedures, the listing itself being non-negotiable. The council was satisfied with the package but the new chairman, Reverend Michael Connolly, expressed surprise that in the past when Yarrabah had pleaded for federal intervention against the Queensland Government for self-management, 'Canberra had its hands tied, but now, to save the trees, Canberra can sweep in and take over Yarrabah'. Yarrabah had decided to 'roll with the punches' because they had no choice.[48] Ironically the central plank of the chequebook settlement of the environmental listing was that the Commonwealth paid for the upgrading of the Yarrabah sawmill.

Secure land title, local control of land, services, and community affairs are necessary, as also is the conversion of social structures and legal rules that match the rhetoric of self-determination. There is need for more realistic debate about the limits of self-determination. Even if we settle for self-management and self-sufficiency, it must mean more than treating Aborigines as if they were poor whites in receipt of government funds in the welfare state. This requires that we overcome what Les Murray describes as 'the most salient and persistent characteristic of white men: they try to run you, to change you, to rule you, and even when they're nice to you, (they) always know better'.

Compensation

'Pay the Rent' is a popular catchcry for urban Aborigines agitating to have land rights flow on to them. Conceding that little land has so far been available for them, they claim compensation for what they have lost.

In the Barunga Statement, Aborigines called for compensation 'for the loss of use of our lands, there having been no extinction of original title'. Though Mr Clyde Holding when minister had promised to negotiate compensation for lost land, nothing was included in the preferred land rights model. Mr Hawke and his later ministers have steered clear of the compensation question. During the 1990 federal election campaign, Marshall Perron, Chief Minister of the Northern Territory, wrote to Prime Minister Hawke asking whether his proposed treaty would 'include a clause which specifies national compensation payments to Aboriginal people for loss of land and social and cultural disruption'. He enquired where the money would come from, and in particular whether the government would levy a national Aboriginal compensation tax.[49] Hawke did not reply. Perron told the NT legislature that 'every Territorian and every Australian is owed a clear unequivocal explanation from the Labor Party on where it stands'. Seeking to flush out a response, he accused Labor politicians of raising the treaty 'as a palliative, a cargo cult compensation promise which can only mislead Aboriginal Australians':

I am convinced that while compensation talk helps Labor win Aboriginal votes, the treaty itself will never come to pass.

The Greek community, and the Italian community for example, the Europeans whose numbers built up through post-war migration, and our Chinese and other communities – will they readily agree to having to foot a bill the size of which Labor refuses to tell us? I doubt it.

To get over this, some proponents of a treaty say compensation is not part of the plan. Who are they trying to fool?

Compensation has always been on the agenda because, why have a treaty if you can't get something tangible from it?[50]

Still the Prime Minister remained silent. Meanwhile the Government had informed the Working Group on Indigenous Populations in Geneva that it could not agree to a declaration that provided payment of compensation for lost lands. Hawke has never envisaged the payment of lump sums or annuities to Aborigines for lands lost in the past. Whatever tangible results are to flow from the instrument of reconciliation, they are not in the form of monetary compensation. This was implicit in the ALP's parliamentary response to Perron's ministerial statement. Aboriginal Labor member, Stanley Tipiloura, argued that:

'compensate' means 'to make up for, make amends for, make equal returns to', etc. It does not necessarily mean money. When you talk about 'compensate', you do not necessarily mean money.

The Chief Minister proposes that compensation means direct cash pay-outs to individuals. That is what he came out with in his statement. He thinks that money is everything. His statement says nothing about creating jobs and things like that.

Compensation does not necessarily mean money. It means the creation of jobs, health services and so on. The policy clearly refers to 'appropriate compensation' and if members opposite cannot understand that, there must be something wrong with them ... We are going to help these people by setting up good jobs for them, trying to provide funds for them, and providing better housing and water services. That is all there is. We are not necessarily worried about giving them money.[51]

The other Aboriginal ALP member, Wesley Lanhupuy, said on talkback radio the next morning that compensation was an issue to be discussed:

Compensation itself is a matter of not only looking in cash terms or in rental terms – there are other areas of compensation – for example, to raise the standard of living, education and equality and also social justice for Aboriginal people.

Cash payments for lost lands will not be on the agenda for the proposed instrument. Dr Hewson has told Mr Hawke: 'we would be opposed' to 'an obligation for compensation'.[52] A distinction needs to be made between welfare and affirmative action programmes and compensation. Measures such as the Aboriginal secondary school grants scheme (Abstudy) are justified not because of Aboriginal dispossession in the past, but because of disadvantage in the present. Before that scheme was introduced, the retention rate to Year 12 of Australian children identified in the census as Aboriginal was very low. This target group was offered special assistance so as to accelerate their access to equal opportunity in Australian society. In 1976 there were only 177 Aborigines in Year 12 throughout the whole of Australia. With the scheme in full swing, this increased to 882 in a decade. The number in secondary education had doubled and the retention rate from Year 8 to 12 had trebled. The fact that the target group is made up of descendants of those dispossessed and dispersed from their lands is incidental.

The scheme does not compensate dispossession; it assists members of an identifiable target group who have not had a fair go measurable against outcomes for the average citizen.

The provision of government funds for the purchase of land to be vested in dispossessed Aboriginal groups is an instance of compensation. The funds are provided to these groups, and not to other Australians without a land base, so as to compensate them for what they have lost. For example, the New South Wales Land Rights Act 1983 provides for a fixed percentage of land tax to be expended on Aboriginal land purchases. The preamble of that Act acknowledged that the land was traditionally owned and occupied by Aborigines and that as a result of past government decisions the amount of land set aside for Aborigines was progressively reduced without compensation. The compensation is not assessed according to the value of lost land nor to the equity that individuals would now enjoy if community lands had not been confiscated. The compensation is a notional amount governed by budgetary considerations and limited by public acceptance.

If cash payments to individuals were to be contemplated, there would have to be a strict formula applied to identify lands lost and to calculate individual entitlements according to racial criteria, which could be demeaning as well as uncertain. Given the racial mix of Aborigines who no longer live on their traditional lands, it would be impossible to devise a national formula and very difficult to finalise the thousands of local agreements that would be needed.

Local Treaties

One attempt to draw up local agreements was made by Aborigines living on Stradbroke Island in 1989. Members of the Nunukul–Ngugi Cultural Heritage Aboriginal Corporation of Quandamooka drew up a draft treaty claiming

Stradbroke Island as their traditional land. They circulated it together with a draft lease agreement to landholders on the island.[53]

At Stradbroke, some people came from Moreton Island and some from the mainland, and intermarried with the traditional owners. The drafters of the treaty decided not to identify the traditional lands of the Nunukul and of the Ngugi separately. If they had, it may have resulted in some individuals being parties to several treaties. Where there had been an occupation of one group's traditional land by an Aboriginal group from elsewhere, there may also have been a need for a treaty between those groups. This would have raised a problem with people who were descended from both groups.

Though placing two or more Aboriginal groups together as a single contracting party may be neater and simpler, it does highlight the moral complexity and uncertainty of the process two centuries after the mixing of peoples has occurred with no regard for land boundaries. In this situation a person's race is an indicator of dispossession and ongoing loss. At the same time there are many people who are descended from those we might call the vanquishers as well as the vanquished. It is difficult to see how their identification with the vanquished and acceptance by the local community could be sufficient to give rise to a moral claim against others, particularly if that claim is to carry a right to monetary compensation paid on the basis of race.

The other party to proposed local treaties or leases would presumably include the recently arrived migrant whose forebears did not dispossess Aborigines of anything. And some of those claiming compensation are descendants themselves from the most ruthless vanquishers of our colonial history, including the cattle kings. On what grounds should the recent migrant or some group of which he or she is a member be obliged personally to pay rent or compensation to another group of citizens who include descendants of the vanquishers?

It is 200 years too late for legally enforceable agreements creating individual entitlements on the basis of race. Rather what is needed is a charter that recognises the collective entitlement of Aboriginal groups to self-management and self-determination, to be funded by society at large in pursuit of the common good.

If Aboriginal leaders are prepared to abandon the rhetoric of sovereignty and if Aborigines generally want to see themselves as citizens of a sovereign nation, Australia, there may be the possibility of negotiating an agreement with them about the terms of their participation in the life of the nation. That could be done in good faith only after their outstanding land claims had been addressed and their continued disadvantage in society rectified. Then the Commonwealth Parliament and Government should take the initiative of calling the States to the table to participate in consultations and negotiations aimed at maximising the possibility of Aboriginal communities managing their own affairs and determining their future in the life of the Australian nation. The outcome should provide for some review process of government actions – a process which the majority of Australians including Aborigines could claim as their own. Searching for options, politicians have spoken of a treaty and now an instrument of reconciliation. The limits of what is achievable can be set down in light of the history of recent treaty talk.

TWO:
TREATY TALK BEFORE 1988

The preamble of the Commonwealth of Australia Constitution Act commences with the words: 'Whereas people of the Australian colonies, humbly relying on the blessing of Almighty God, have agreed to unite in one indissoluble Commonwealth'. No agreements, however, had been sought from Aborigines in those colonies. Until the 1967 referendum Aborigines could not be counted in determining the size of electorates for the House of Representatives. They were irrelevant to the democratic basis of our constitution.

In 1974 Senator Neville Bonner, the first Aboriginal member of the Commonwealth Parliament, introduced a resolution in the Senate:

That the Senate accepts the fact that the indigenous people of Australia, now known as Aborigines and Torres Strait Islanders, were in possession of this entire nation prior to the 1788 First Fleet landing at Botany Bay, urges the Australian Government to admit prior ownership by the said indigenous people, and introduce legislation to compensate the people now known as Aborigines and Torres Strait Islanders for dispossession of their land.[1]

After some months on the notice paper, the resolution was passed on the voices with no debate.

In April 1979, the National Aboriginal Conference (NAC), which was an elected body of Aborigines set up by the Fraser Government, decided to work for a 'Treaty of

Commitment'. The treaty discussion has been on and off the political agenda ever since.

In the same month, the fourteen member Aboriginal Treaty Committee chaired by Dr H. C. Coombs held its first meeting.[2] Senator Fred Chaney, then Liberal Minister for Aboriginal Affairs, welcomed the NAC initiatives on the treaty. Chaney spoke of the Government's willingness to join any discussions as the proposal progressed and Prime Minister Malcolm Fraser agreed to meet the NAC executive. In light of more recent statements on the treaty by the Liberal and National Parties, it is worth noting that at that time there was no threat to tear up any proposal. After discussing the matter with the NAC executive, Fraser indicated to them that his minister, Fred Chaney, was examining the proposal and would be bringing it to the Government for consideration. Fraser was committed to a policy of self-management and hoped the NAC would develop into a national umbrella body for Aboriginal organisations in order to provide accessable advice to the Commonwealth Government on policy in Aboriginal Affairs. Nine years later, Chaney revealed that as a minister, he was extremely active in discouraging the idea of an Aboriginal treaty on the grounds that it was socially and politically divisive.[3]

The NAC issued an interim report on the treaty proposal in July 1980 after an initial consultation tour. The Central Australian Aboriginal Congress asked that no action be taken until an Aboriginal consensus had emerged. The congress thought this would take at least five years. They would not agree to anything until it had been ratified by the people.[4]

When Chaney was promoted into Cabinet, Senator Peter Baume took over as Minister for Aboriginal Affairs. Chaney had been labelled 'Red Fred' for his modest espousal of the Aboriginal cause in the unsympathetic Western Australian Liberal Party. Baume, a Jewish medical academic from Sydney, brought continued dedication and liberal sentiment to the portfolio. He told the NAC that 'any agreement must reflect the special place of Aboriginal and Torres Strait Islander people within Australian society as part of one Australian nation'. The NAC conceded there were difficulties that could be avoided if the word 'treaty' could be replaced. They had chosen a Yolngu word 'makarrata', which signified 'the end of a dispute between communities and the resumption of normal relations'.[5] Baume said the NAC had 'itself helped to settle this important area of concern'.

Having clarified that he did not use the word 'treaty' 'for reasons which have to do with the precise legal meaning of the word', Baume set out the Government's position in March 1981:

The Government proposes, with the help of the National Aboriginal Conference, to pursue the concept of a makarrata and also to provide assistance to the NAC to research and develop the proposal. In doing so, the Government is prepared to acknowledge prior occupation of Australia by Aboriginals. We are not prepared to act unilaterally in those areas where the States have an interest. I have indicated to the NAC in a number of particular matters that the Government cannot negotiate a treaty which implies an internationally recognised agreement between two nations. I have indicated to the NAC that the Government cannot agree to any fixed financial commitment in the future. I have also indicated to the NAC that the Government cannot support the proposal for reserved seats in the Parliament for Aboriginals. I have also indicated in response to a particular recommendation from the NAC that the Government does not believe that a system where Aboriginal employment is subject to a rigidly fixed formula is appropriate. Nevertheless the Government has indicated a position from which it will negotiate. The Aboriginal representatives have now opened up the matter further with the State governments. It is up to them to take the next step.[6]

Though a list of largely negative parameters, it assured Aboriginal representatives of the Government's commitment to negotiate while also providing some idea of the limits. The Liberals saw State Governments as central to the negotiation process from the outset. Trying to get a firmer handle on what financial and legal issues were negotiable with the Fraser Government, Senator Susan Ryan asked for a timetable and process for negotiation. Senator Baume gave little away but he did say that he had agreement from several States to negotiate with the NAC.[7]

The third assembly of the World Council of Indigenous Peoples was held in Canberra in April 1981. This international organisation was set up to give indigenous people throughout the world a network and a voice in UN organisations. The assembly provided a forum for a range of Australian Aboriginal viewpoints. Kevin Gilbert, a noted Aboriginal author, claimed the NAC was 'formulated by and acts under the auspices of the Australian Government'. In turn, the NAC presented a position paper to the council stating its difference of view with the Australian Government about the makarrata:

We the Aboriginal people plainly think of it as a treaty with the Aboriginal nation . . . [The government] hopes to have the Aborigines accept from the outset of the negotiations . . . that they are part of the Australian nation as a whole.

In September 1981 (just before the Commonwealth Heads of Government Meeting was to take place in Sydney and Canberra), the Senate referred the whole question to the Standing Committee on Constitutional and Legal Affairs, which did not report until well after the Hawke Government came to power in 1983. NAC representatives had attended a meeting of the Australian Aboriginal Affairs Council in March 1981 so as to outline the makarrata proposals to State governments. They put further proposals for the process and content of a makarrata to the

Government on 29 September 1981 and 1 October 1981, as a follow-up to the interim report they had submitted after their initial round of consultations in July 1980.

During the lead up to the 1982 Commonwealth Games in Brisbane, Baume was replaced by Ian Bonython Wilson, who unlike his two predecessors had almost no involvement with Aborigines before coming to the portfolio. Under pressure to clarify the Government's position on the makarrata before the games, he said it was impossible to agree to many of the demands the NAC had presented. In its formal submissions to the Senate Standing Committee on Constitutional and Legal Affairs during 1982, the NAC was resolute in claiming that separate Aboriginal nationhood and sovereignty were non-negotiable starting points, asserting 'our basic rights as sovereign Aboriginal nations who are equal in political status with the Commonwealth of Australia'.[8] But there was confusion in the rhetoric. The same submission was concluded with an awareness of the 'Australian ambition to be one nation, one people' and 'eagerness to come to terms with these negotiations in a satisfactory manner which will not cause unnecessary political wrangles'.[9] In a supplementary submission, the makarrata sub-committee of the NAC reaffirmed the central concern 'that Aboriginal communities wish to be recognised as sovereign nations capable of governing themselves'. They were then considering three possibilities:

1 International sovereignty, perhaps introduced through a period of trusteeship;
2 The creation of an additional state within the Commonwealth governed by Aboriginal and Torres Strait Islander people within current constitutional structures;
3 The creation of self-governing regions within the Commonwealth comprised of self-governing communities involving powers of local self-government.[10]

The Senate referred the matter to the Standing

Committee on Constitutional and Legal Affairs, which did not report until after the election of the Hawke Government. Before developing the Commonwealth's position, Wilson wished to await the Senate Committee report, which was not expected until early 1983. But he reconfirmed the Government's interest in pursuing the makarrata once the NAC had finalised its proposals, adding that 'the Government does not believe that it is appropriate for the Commonwealth to tell the NAC what it should include in its proposals'.[11]

With the international spotlight on Queensland during the 1982 Commonwealth Games, Premier Joh Bjelke-Petersen put forward some very modest proposals for land rights and self-management of Queensland communities. The Fraser Government was constrained by its commitment to State rights and was unable to rectify this shortfall with the result that the ALP Opposition took up the cry for reform and pledged national legislation if elected in Canberra. In opposition, the Shadow Minister Senator Susan Ryan took the rare step of introducing into the Senate a doomed self-management Bill for Queensland reserves as a symbol of Labor's commitment.

It was a division of Aboriginal opinion rather than Government opposition to the makarrata that allowed it to come off the political agenda. All the Government had to do was sit on its hands. The NAC itself was on the slippery road to oblivion. The better resourced land councils were more concerned with land rights than treaties. Other local Aboriginal organisations were more concerned with the daily management of services to their communities.

Elected in March 1983, the Hawke Government made cautious attempts to implement its bold party platform on land rights. Clyde Holding became the nation's longest serving Minister for Aboriginal Affairs and devoted much of his administration to a proposal for national land rights. This proposal ultimately came unstuck in Western Australia, where the State Labor Government was unwilling to give Aborigines a veto over mining on their land, in the face of well-resourced opposition from the mining industry. It was even more unwilling to have a Federal Government of the same political hue intervene in what was seen as a State issue to deliver land title to Aborigines in the face of a hostile upper house in the State Parliament. In the early days of the proposed national land rights, the Federal Government thought that Aborigines in the Northern Territory may be prepared to do a trade-off, forfeiting their own limited veto power in return for land gains being made by Aborigines in the States where State Governments had moved slowly or not at all.

After the failure of national land rights, Holding handed the baton to Gerry Hand whose administration of the portfolio was dedicated to establishing the Aboriginal and Torres Strait Islander Commission (ATSIC) and responding to criticism about the accountability of Aboriginal organisations. Hundreds of questions were placed on notice at Senate Estimates Committees by Senator Tambling, which ultimately resulted in stricter accountability of Aboriginal organisations. Though Labor ministers have had to spend much of their time putting out bushfires and attending to only one major policy initiative at a time, whether it be national land rights or ATSIC, the treaty has been a recurring theme throughout the Hawke administration. Once ATSIC was established, Minister Robert Tickner was able to devote more time to the concept, by then defined as the instrument of reconciliation.

At the time of its election to Government, the ALP had a strong policy commitment to national land rights. It had also made a commitment to 'investigate the principle of a Treaty of Commitment as negotiated on other continents to set out the legal and cultural relationships between the Aboriginal and Islander peoples and the wider Australian community, a treaty process'.[12]

Two months after the election, Senator Gareth Evans, the Attorney-General, was cautious in telling the Senate that his party would favourably consider a treaty if it were supported by Aborigines generally.[13] Then the Senate Standing Committee on Constitutional and Legal Affairs tabled its report. Five of the committee members (Senators Gareth Evans, Susan Ryan, Nick Bolkus, Peter Cook, and Michael Tate) were to become ministers in the Hawke Government. The committee unanimously rejected the idea of an international treaty as unreal. They concluded:

[As] a legal proposition, the sovereignty is not now vested in the Aboriginal peoples except insofar as they share in the common sovereignty of all peoples of the Commonwealth of Australia. In particular, they are not a sovereign entity under our present law, so that they cannot enter into a treaty with the Commonwealth.[14]

It was common ground for all senators that it was too late for a treaty in the strict sense. There were no longer two distinct parties recognised in international law who could negotiate and finalise a treaty. The Senate Committee recommended instead that the Government, in consultation with Aboriginal groups, consider inserting a provision in the constitution 'which would confer a broad power on the Commonwealth to enter into a compact with representatives of the Aboriginal people'.[15]

This process would require a constitutional amendment, consultations and negotiation with a national Aboriginal representative body and detailed legislation. There was no quick solution. The committee saw a need for education of Aboriginal communities about the concept before there could be any realistic negotiations. The committee also recommended 'a continuing and extended education programme occurring in the non-Aboriginal community, so that by the time the compact is ready to be concluded, a valuable process of healing and understanding between both communities will have taken place'.[16]

Tabling the report, Senator Tate had emphasised 'that the committee's terms of reference did not require it to come to a conclusion as to the desirability or usefulness of the makarrata concept'. That was to be decided at another time, by other people. But he did add the caveat: 'Clearly such an agreement would only succeed if it were understood and supported throughout the whole Australian community.'[17] And the evidence before the committee indicated a widespread lack of information and understanding about the concept. Any makarrata was to be a long time coming, if ever. Senator Robert Hill (later to become Leader of the Liberal Party in the Senate) had also served on the committee and told the Senate that on a moral basis, 'the descendants of the original inhabitants have a good case for compensation or reparation as having been wrongly dispossessed'. He thought the form of reparation had to be consistent 'with the overall goal of building a strong, united, just Australia' and had firmed in his view 'that the concept of makarrata is not a prerequisite to achieving such goals and in fact it involves so many extraneous difficulties that it might be counter-productive'.[18] Attorney-General Evans had by this time not only rejected the word 'treaty' but also the word 'compact' to describe the legal instrument that might be contemplated.

On the last sitting day before Labor's first Christmas in Government, Clyde Holding introduced a motion to the House of Representatives entitled 'Aboriginal Past: Australia's Future'. By convention, such statements are usually given to the Opposition at least two hours before presentation to allow decent debate. The Opposition was given only one hour's notice of this lengthy statement, thereby engendering suspicion about the Government's motives. The motion set out five principles necessary for land rights:

1 Aboriginal land to be held under inalienable freehold;
2 Protection of sacred sites;
3 Aboriginal control in relation to mining on Aboriginal land;

4 Access to mining royalty equivalents;
5 Compensation for lost land to be negotiated.

The motion also acknowledged that 'from the time of arrival of representatives of King George III of England, and subsequent conquest of the land and the subjugation of the Aboriginal people, no settlement was concluded between those representatives and the Aboriginal and Torres Strait Islander people'.[19]

Though pledging co-operation with co-operative State Governments, Holding told Parliament: 'No one should be in any doubt. Although this is a government of national reconciliation and although we seek harmony in our relations with the States, the demands of Aboriginal people for justice will no longer be denied.'[20] Throwing down the gauntlet, he proclaimed: 'The human rights of Aboriginal and Islander Australians must take precedence over state rights.'

Looking ahead to 1988, he said: 'We must understand the past, which we cannot change, in order to build the future. But we must not repeat the hypocrisy. We must not make only cosmetic changes merely for the sake of the bicentennial celebrations.'[21]

By this time, some Aboriginal leaders were attending international meetings on indigenous rights, discussing treaty ideas far beyond the modest proposals being entertained by the ALP. Marcia Langton had recently returned from a meeting of the Working Group on Indigenous Populations, which was to report to the Sub-Commission on Prevention of Discrimination and Protection of Minorities. She had attended on behalf of the Federation of Land Councils and was encouraging other organisations to attend future meetings. A fortnight before Holding introduced his resolution to Parliament, the Aboriginal Treaty Committee dissolved itself and committed its last funds to a conference on Aborigines and International Law. The conference was co-sponsored by the major national

Aboriginal organisations. In a report on her trip, Marcia Langton asserted that Holding was 'labouring under the confused notion that Aboriginal organisations other than the National Aboriginal Conference should not speak in international fora'. Paul Coe spoke on sovereignty and power, saying that the first concept might be 'over our heads' but that the latter was understood by everyone. He could not see any reason why there could not be three sovereign bodies under the Australian umbrella: the Aboriginal nation, the Commonwealth Government and the State Governments. He suggested that the Aboriginal nation should also be eligible for a fixed share of the GNP. Holding had attended the conference and stated from the outset that sovereignty for Aborigines was out of the question. Whatever was intended by the Hawke Government, there was never any suggestion of recognition of Aboriginal sovereignty. In his ministerial statement Holding told the Parliament that he had:

> made it clear to Aboriginal people that neither the grant of land rights, nor recognition of Aboriginal prior occupation and ownership, in any way puts Australian sovereignty in question. Given the opportunity, Aboriginal people will make their own future as citizens of the Australian nation, as we all shall. Sovereignty is vested in the Crown and Parliaments, for a single people united in the Commonwealth. The people who are so united under the Crown are all Australians. These matters are not in question.[22]

After Christmas, Holding's land rights motion was allowed to lapse. Cabinet did not consider the matter. Later in the year there was an election back in the air. As usual, the Government went quiet on Aboriginal issues once it had moved into election mode. However, Holding did repeat much of the motion in his address to the United Nations Working Group on Indigenous Populations. Though not debated in Parliament nor approved by Cabinet, the motion was held out to the international community as a statement of Government policy.

During the 1984 election campaign, Hawke confirmed that his Government had no intention of overriding the Western Australian Labor Government's decision not to permit an Aboriginal veto over mining or exploration on land in that State. He argued: 'We don't believe that the right of veto is an integral part of having effective, fair and efficient land rights legislation.'[23] The Commonwealth Government had by this time received a confidential report from the Australian National Opinion Poll showing that support for land rights was very low. Without reference to the report, Hawke announced:

If we are as Australians going to have the people of Australia reflecting now some twenty years later the desire they expressed overwhelmingly in 1967, if we're going to have that working effectively we've got to have an acceptance by the majority of the Australian people that what is being done reflects their wishes and desires ... The worst thing that could happen for the Aboriginal people of Australia and for the Australian community is that there should be imposed unilaterally from Canberra some position which is not accepted by the majority of Australian people in giving effect to the wish they expressed in 1967 for a national position.[24]

Holding released the Preferred National Land Rights Model in February 1985. Three months later, the Government tabled its response to the 1983 Senate report on the treaty proposal:

The Government considers that the concept of Makarrata must be seen in the context of the efforts required to promote community acceptance for the concept of national land rights legislation. The wider issues involved in a Makarrata would make it difficult at this stage to enlist the support necessary to achieve constitutional amendment as recommended by the Committee.[25]

If national land rights was looking hard, a treaty (whatever its legal status) was looking impossible. It had been dropped from the Government's agenda. In August, the Cabinet endorsed the principles of the preferred model but made no commitment for legislation. The day after Cabinet met, Holding made it clear that the Government would proceed with further consultation as a basis for possible Commonwealth legislation, but that the Government's preferred position was 'that land rights be implemented by State action broadly consistent with the Commonwealth's principles rather than by overriding Commonwealth legislation'.[26]

This was hardly an application of the big stick by Canberra. And there were no carrots to be offered. It was an exercise in moral exhortation. Things were to get worse because it was Western Australian Premier Brian Burke's turn to face the polls early in 1986. Robert Tickner, then a new backbencher in the Government, wanted to console people opposed to land rights that they had little to fear. He told Parliament 'that in relation to the Government's national Aboriginal land rights program not one square inch of Australia has ever, under any of the Government's proposals, been the subject of any suggested claim by Aboriginal people'.[27] Two days earlier he had asked Holding what action he had taken to investigate a treaty of commitment that could set out the legal and cultural relationships between Aborigines and other citizens of Western Australia. Holding did not want to know about it. Answering on notice a fortnight later, he said: 'Any Treaty of Commitment between Aboriginal and Islander peoples and the Western Australian community is a matter for Western Australia.'[28] During the Western Australian election campaign, Burke threatened to resign if national land rights legislation were introduced. In response Hawke reassured the Western Australian electors that Burke had nothing to fear.

After the Western Australian election, Holding presented a submission to Federal Cabinet that presumed national legislation would not be introduced and which accom-

modated Burke's promise that there be no new special
Aboriginal land legislation, even at a State level in Western
Australia. Following this, changes were made to the
Commonwealth legislation dealing with Aboriginal land in
the Northern Territory that modified the mining veto
provisions there. The modifications contained more concessions to the mining industry than Justice Toohey had
recommended in his review of the legislation. These
concessions did not have the approval of traditional land
owners and their land councils.

In its first three years in office, the Hawke Government
was besieged by the mining lobby and those State
Governments that did not want to be subjected to a national
regime of Aboriginal rights, especially if these rights could
be exercised adverse to the interests of State development
driven by mineral exploration and exploitation. By March
1986, Holding had to admit defeat. In doing so, he all but
blamed the Aborigines for the failure of the proposal:

I had a specific direction from Cabinet to engage in discussions
with the States to see what action could be taken on a State by
State basis. That position was clear and unequivocal and was well
known to Aboriginal leadership who in many cases rejected the
proposed model.[29]

The Commonwealth had expected Northern Territory
Aborigines to trade their veto over mining on their land for
a Commonwealth undertaking to consult with the States
about Aboriginal land title in State jurisdictions. Despite
Holding's bold remarks when publishing the proposed
model a year earlier, he implied that Commonwealth acquisition of Aboriginal land in a State jurisdiction would have
occurred only if the State government had requested it:

I am sure that it would come as no surprise that no State
Government has suggested to me that the Commonwealth should
take pre-emptive action in this matter.[30]

Putting on a brave face, he told Parliament:

We will continue to negotiate with the States. We will continue to seek to advance the interest of Aboriginal people through co-operation with the States where that is possible. Such an approach does not involve any diminution of Commonwealth responsibility. Aboriginal people enjoy a better outcome, and sooner, in a much better social environment by means of such a process. Against this background of continuing dialogue and progress with the States, the Government has taken the view that the implementation of legislation based on the preferred model is not warranted at this time.[31]

Later Holding claimed that fifty Aboriginal groups had expressed dissatisfaction with the preferred land rights model because it did not go far enough and that was why the Government decided to drop it altogether. Among the criticisms, he mentioned the model's perceived inappropriateness for Aborigines in some circumstances or in particular States, the lack of a mining veto, a lack of adequate protection for sacred sites and the ten year limit on claims.[32]

Because Aborigines were unhappy with the compromised model being proposed, nothing was to be legislated. Given the lack of Aboriginal support for the model and the lack of progress made in the States (that is, a total lack of progress in Tasmania and Western Australia and no appreciable change in the other States since the proposed model was announced in 1985), the Hawke Government walked away from its commitment. The broken promises were the grossest breach of faith committed by any government towards Aboriginal people since white settlement. Never had so much been promised, with absolutely nothing being delivered, and with Aborigines themselves receiving the blame. The necessity 'to find approaches which would advance the interests of Aboriginal Australians while at the same time gaining general acceptability within the overall Australian community', meant that in trying to reconcile these aims, Holding found it was then 'necessary to adopt positions on a number of matters which have resulted in some disappointment to Aboriginal aspirations'.[33] The Northern Territory land councils realised that even with the abandonment of the preferred model, they were still at risk of losing their mining veto. When the dust of Government rhetoric had settled Aborigines were actually to have their legal rights weakened. Later a letter from Hawke to Holding was published which showed how little the national Government was prepared to do in seeking land rights from recalcitrant State Governments. Expressing his unwillingness to acquire compulsorily or to exchange land in Tasmania, Hawke told Holding that 'in any event ... the State should be seen to take the first step so any Commonwealth involvement is clearly in response to a State initiative'.[34]

Holding's last major address as Minister was to the National Press Club on the twentieth anniversary of the 1967 referendum, the day a Federal election was announced. Giving the treaty another run, he said it was 'not surprising that there is renewed interest in the concept of a treaty between Aboriginal and non-Aboriginal Australians. The idea, of course, has been around for some time'.[35] It did not become an election issue. It was neither promoted by the Government nor exploited by the opposition. Launching his campaign at the Opera House, the Prime Minister did not mention Aborigines by name but by implication referred to their plight when he cast his eye towards 1988:

We have Australian achievements, splendid achievements, to celebrate, but we Australians have mistakes to rectify, amends to make, and wrongs to put right if Australia is to achieve its full promise of what it can be, and should be – simply the best and fairest nation on earth.

Re-elected for his third term, Hawke prepared the ground for the last National Aborigines Week before the bicentenary by lending his name and office to the treaty idea. On 2 September 1987, he started his day with an interview at the Central Australian Aboriginal Media Association in Alice Springs, where he proffered an opinion and made a commitment that came as a surprise to everyone, including his minister, Gerry Hand. He thought much could be done in a short time. Asked about recognition for what Aborigines had suffered over the previous 200 years, Hawke responded:

Whenever I speak of the bicentennial I talk about it being a celebration of 200 years of European settlement because we must all remember that ... the most fleeting stage of the history of this country goes back 40 000 years or more. And I very much want to see a situation before 1987 finishes whereby there can be a clear understanding by all of us that that is the case. And I would like to see 1988 preceded by some sort of understanding – compact, if you like, I don't want to get caught up in particular words – but a compact of understanding between the whole Australian community which recognises that 1988 is the celebration of 200 years of European settlement. And to recognise that in that 200 years very many injustices have been suffered by the Aboriginal people ...

But that compact, or statement of understanding, should recognise that there is an obligation and commitment on the part of the whole Australian community to move further in the areas of education, health, employment, training so that there can be confidence in the Aboriginal community as we go into 1988, that the proper celebrations that there should be of the bicentenary in the sense that I have described it, is something which they can identify.[36]

Then he was asked about a treaty:

Whether it is called a treaty, I am open-minded about that. I don't think we should be hung up on words – a treaty, a compact. The important thing is that there be a clear statement of understanding by the total Australian community of the obligations that the community has to rectify some of the injustices that have occurred during our 200 years . . . statement of understanding, of obligation, and of commitment, those are the important things.

The discussion then turned to land rights and he repeated his co-operative federalism line, hinting that national land rights was dead and buried:

We have taken the view that what is fundamentally important if we are going to make negotiations and meaningful decisions about land rights stick is that we have as much support as we can from the people in government in the states because the worst thing that could happen . . . would be if there was an attempt just quickly and unilaterally to impose something from the centre . . . we, when we came to office in 1983, developed broad principles in regard to Aboriginal land rights and then decided that what we would want to do would be to negotiate with each of the states.

So even in this first interview, the Prime Minister was not promising anything radical. In fact he was confining himself to a statement that would have no legal effect, which would not interfere with Federal–State relations, and which would have nothing to do with land rights. He then arrived at the airport to be besieged by journalists who had missed the 'treaty story'. He repeated himself, saying the word was not important but the concept was. There was a need for a compact of understanding so everyone could enjoy 1988. He thought it could all be achieved by placing 'a substantial preamble' in the forthcoming ATSIC legislation. On the subject of the treaty, he now said: 'the treaty doesn't appeal to me so much – but it is not the word that matters.' Two questions later he responded at greater length:

The rights of Aborigines should be enshrined in the laws of this country . . . and we do this in many ways already. In the areas of specific programmes for housing and employment and so on. And I am not in saying that implying that we have done enough but the concept of having an overall treaty, I don't know that that is necessarily the right way or the necessary way to do it.

He and the media flew on to Katherine. The national media had gone into a feeding frenzy on 'the treaty' by this stage. Next day, he and Gerry Hand gave a joint press conference. Asked if he would be prepared to accept a treaty as opposed to a compact 'if it really comes to a crunch', he replied that he did not think 'we should be creating unreal expectations by using a word now which may have connotations that are inappropriate or undeliverable'.

By this time, he was getting very testy on the question of a treaty's ramifications. He did not want to become involved in questions about compensation for lost land and separate sovereignty.

Charles Perkins, Secretary of the Department of Aboriginal Affairs, had bought into the discussion, calling for a treaty that could be written into the constitution. The modesty of the Prime Minister's hopes for outcomes from the process was revealed in his restating the suggestion 'that the concept could be embedded into legislation as part of the preamble' of the ATSIC legislation. He did not want to rouse 'undue expectations' by use of the word treaty. But for the opposition's fear tactics, it is hard to see how he could have roused any expectations at all. All he wanted was an acknowledgement of the facts of history agreed to by all parties.

This was to be achieved despite the abolition of the National Aboriginal Conference, which had not been replaced by any national elected body. Things were further complicated by the National Coalition of Aboriginal Organisations (established in May 1986) having circulated a draft treaty written by Kevin Gilbert, which was to be 'executed between us, the Sovereign People of This Our Land, Australia, and the Non-Aboriginal Peoples who invaded and colonised our lands'. Perkins, described the document's key terms as 'ludicrous, nonsensical and childlike'. They may well have been, but the document was the only thing in existence that gave some idea of what some Aborigines understood by the Government's sporadic treaty utterances. The Aboriginal division about its contents had no forum in which to resolve itself. There was no prospect of any agreement being negotiated in the foreseeable future, let alone before the magical date of 26 January 1988.

Stan Tipaloura, an Aboriginal Labor member of the Northern Territory Legislative Assembly, accepted an appointment to the board of the Bicentennnial Authority and said that he would bring to the notice of the board the need for a constitutionally recognised treaty between Aboriginal and non-Aboriginal Australians. He conceded: 'It may not all come together by 1988, but it must start somewhere and it takes two sides to work things out.'[37] Speaking of the compact and the bicentennial celebrations after the *Bulletin* carried the Aboriginal criticism that he was an Uncle Tom for accepting such an appointment, he told the Northern Territory Legislative Assembly:

We do not want apartheid. We do not want that. It is not the way we want to live. We know what goes on on the other side of the world ... We are all human beings. Let's develop this place and understand each other instead of being misled by journalists or the media. We have to start acting together ...

[Honourable members opposite] should not just go off the rails with all sorts of comments because of the likes of Michael Mansell.[38]

The *Bulletin* article canvassed a variety of Aboriginal viewpoints on the treaty. Galarrwuy Yunupingu spoke of constitutional guarantees for restoration of land under secure title and the recognition of legitimate sovereignty.

Marcia Langton said the treaty must 'at the very least give to Aboriginal people a special place politically in Australian society'. Shirley McPherson pushed for recognition of prior ownership, 'but at the very least prior occupation and dispossession'. Charles Perkins wanted the treaty enshrined in the constitution but was very critical of Aborigines who were demanding billions of dollars in compensation and vast areas of land: 'It undermines our cause. But it also gives racist governments an opportunity to opt out, as they did with the national land rights legislation.'[39]

The thirty-fifth Parliament of the Commonwealth was opened by the Governor General, Sir Ninian Stephen on 14 September 1987. In his address he said:

The Government believes it is essential, as we come to the Bicentennial year, to recognise that 200 years of European settlement come after 40 000 years of Aboriginal history. The Government will explore how best to reflect that recognition and the obligation which this involves for the whole community.[40]

On 6 October 1987 the *Sydney Morning Herald* published an opinion poll that showed that 58 per cent of those surveyed supported the compact proposal in principle. During question time the next day, the opposition asked the Prime Minister to concede that he had fuelled 'impractical demands and unrealistic expectations in sections of the Aboriginal community by his reckless, off the cuff floating of a proposal for a compact with the Aborigines'. He was also asked to detail the concessions that a compact should contain. He denied that his statement at the Alice Springs radio station the previous month was off the cuff. Detailing no concessions, he spoke of the need for Australians to 'go into 1988 with a sense of shared commitment on the part of the non-Aboriginal people and a recognition that in those 200 years many injustices have been done to the Aboriginal people'. He thought it obvious 'that in such a consideration the representatives of the

Aboriginal people themselves will make demands and suggestions that to us may seem outrageous'.[41] Mr Hawke appeared content with the ambiguity that while he was intending only a statement of facts that would have no legal ramifications, many Aborigines including Charles Perkins, the Commonwealth's most senior Aboriginal bureaucrat, were demanding an instrument with legal effect. Mr Hawke gave no guidance as to what demands would be outrageous and what concessions would be properly considered by his government.

On Parliament's last sitting day before 1988, Gerry Hand made a statement in the House of Representatives entitled 'Foundations for the Future'. He outlined a comprehensive programme for reform aimed at providing Aborigines with 'the means, as never before, to determine their own future as part of this nation'. The cornerstone of the new national edifice for Aboriginal administration was to be the Aboriginal and Torres Strait Islander Commission (ATSIC). Hand took the compact idea one step further by proposing a series of discussions in 1988. He said the name of the agreement, whether compact, agreement, treaty or makarrata, was not significant. He preferred the term compact and made it crystal clear that the Hawke Government, like the Fraser Government, had no intention of negotiating a treaty that would imply an internationally recognised agreement between two nations. The purpose of the exercise was to confront the challenge of building 'a new and lasting era of mutual understanding and co-operation with our Aboriginal and Torres Strait Islander fellow citizens'. He made it clear that national land rights was a dream of the past.

Much of Hand's energy during his term as Minister for Aboriginal Affairs was absorbed in the ATSIC debate and the numerous parliamentary reviews of the administration of Aboriginal affairs. Much energy was wasted on a lengthy preamble to the ATSIC legislation, which was ultimately dropped altogether. He had to put the treaty idea on the back-burner.

THREE:
FROM 1988 TO 2001

'Living Together' in 1988

Mr Hawke made several attempts during 1988 to sow the seed of the treaty idea. He commenced his attempts to include Aborigines in the year's celebrations with his speech at the National Press Club on 22 January 1988. He set out his philosophy of the bicentenary, seeing it as a decisive point in 'the process of national identity, national responsibility and national maturity', accompanied by a reassessment of the past, which would be of greatest value to Aboriginal people. He warned that his Government's commitment to Aborigines was not simply 'some sort of window dressing for the Bicentenary, for consumption overseas'. He developed what was to become a recurrent theme in his declarations about the treaty:

Nor is the [Aboriginal] cause advanced by attempts to draw up an indictment of criminality against the entire Australian nation. The Australian people should never be asked to accept that their entire history as a modern nation must be predicated on the notion of a collective and irredeemable guilt.

In his Australia Day message Hawke pledged 'the Australian Government and the Australian people to an earnest and continuing effort of rectification and reconciliation'. Though giving no outline of process, he did implicitly concede that it would take more than a few months. The quick-fix approach that had been tried before National Aborigines Week the previous year was abandoned. In Hyde Park later in the day, Galarrwuy Yunupingu spoke for the Aborigines of the Northern Territory who had come to dance and celebrate the survival of their culture during 200 turbulent years. He said Aborigines had come from all around Australia in the hope of establishing a future for Australia that 'is very simple and clear – white Australia together with Aboriginal Australians, and then we are all Australians'.

The Shadow Minister for Aboriginal Affairs, Chris Miles, issued an Australia Day statement committing the Opposition to reconciliation. Conceding that many Aborigines feel a sense of alienation 'because of what they see as a lack of acceptance by other Australians', he admitted a responsibility 'to seek unity through reconciliation'. Claiming that Aboriginal alienation could not be reduced 'by appeasement or the rearrangement of bureaucratic structures' he said the Coalition was 'keen to improve relationships between Aboriginal and other Australians and for this reason will firmly oppose a treaty', which would undermine the unity and cohesion of the Australian people and nation. The stage had been reached where Government and Opposition agreed on ends but thought the treaty process would have diametrically opposed results.

After the tall ships and fireworks had come to an end, attention turned to Queensland, where Expo 88 was being held in Brisbane. Aboriginal communities had responded differently to offers of financial assistance from the Commonwealth–State Bicentennial Commemorative Programme. The Aboriginal community in Rockhampton accepted almost $500 000 for their Aboriginal Cultural Centre. At the opening, in April 1988, Mr Hawke took the opportunity to further the treaty discussion another step. Conceding the difficulties with consultation, he sought guidance from his minister, Mr Hand, who 'stressed that the first step towards establishing such an agreement is for

Aboriginal people to convey to the Government their view on how the process of discussing the concept should be set in place'. With no replacement for the abolished NAC and only an under-resourced, little publicised National Coalition of Aboriginal Organisations, it was hard to see how advice on the process could be obtained.

Mr Hawke put the weight of his office behind the treaty proposal at the ALP Conference in the first week of June 1988. He moved a resolution affirming the Government's desire to reach a proper and lasting reconciliation through a compact or treaty so as 'to restate the commitment of the ALP to finding a more mature and lasting relationship between the Aboriginal and the non-Aboriginal people of this country'. Mr Hawke told delegates:

I've never been hung up on the word. The word is unimportant but it's the process which matters. We must work towards some form of agreement in which the essential processes of reconciliation can and will take place. There is no doubt that the bicentenary provides us with a golden opportunity to start serious work towards such an agreement.

Armed with the support of the national conference, the Prime Minister and his wife took off for an Aboriginal sports and culture festival to be held at Barunga in the Northern Territory. There traditional Aboriginal leaders had their own plans for him. He sat down with them, agreed to a five point process, and signed a memorandum with his Minister and Aboriginal elders, Galarrwuy Yunupingu and Wenten Rabuntja:

1 The Government affirms that it is committed to work for a negotiated Treaty with Aboriginal people.
2 The Government sees the next step as Aborigines deciding what they believe should be in the Treaty.
3 The Government will provide the necessary support for Aboriginal people to carry out their own consultations

and negotiations: this could include the formation of a Committee of seven senior Aborigines to oversee the process and to call an Australia-wide meeting or Convention.

4 When the Aborigines present their proposals the Government stands ready to negotiate about them.

5 The Government hopes that these negotiations can commence before the end of 1988 and will lead to an agreed Treaty in the life of this Parliament.

The treaty talk, together with television images of the Prime Minister looking up to Mr Yunupingu in traditional dress sent the Opposition into another flurry about the word 'treaty'. Mr Howard responded by way of a press release:

The notion is utterly repugnant to the ideal of one Australia. It is an absurd proposition for a nation to make a treaty with some of its citizens.

Such a treaty is a leap into the Constitutional unknown. It will become a Constitutional nightmare. It raises implications of legal interpretation which could be quite horrendous.[1]

In January of the bicentennial year fourteen heads of Australian Christian Churches issued a statement entitled 'Towards Reconciliation in Australian Society'. It focussed on the history of Aboriginal–European contact and conflict, the place of Aborigines in Australian society and the need for committed acts of reconciliation.

The church leaders recommended that, as a symbolic action, the Commonwealth Parliament:

Make formal acknowledgement of the nation's Aboriginal prehistory and the enduring place of our Aboriginal heritage. Our parliamentarians could do this if they were to pass unanimously a suitable resolution which could be acknowledged by the Queen at the opening of the new Parliament House on 9 May 1988.[2]

A working text of a resolution had been sent to politicians in October 1987. It was formally submitted to the Prime Minister, Mr Hawke, and the Leader of the Opposition, Mr Howard, two weeks after publication of the church leaders' statement. Initially, neither the Government nor Opposition was much interested in seeking a bipartisan approach stating what was common ground. Eventually a resolution was passed through both houses of Parliament as the first item of substantive business in the new Parliament House, but without Opposition support. However, Howard did tell Parliament that both the Liberal and National Parties had a genuine desire 'to be associated with a sensible bipartisan motion on this issue'.[3] He said that the party's only difficulty was with the paragraph that referred to self-management and self-determination. This eleventh-hour concern was all that stood in the way of a unanimous resolution. The original resolution had already been amended to accommodate Opposition concerns. In its final form, the resolution read:

That the House of Representatives/Senate –
1 ackowledges that:
    a) Australia was occupied by Aborigines and Torres Strait Islanders who had settled for thousands of years before British settlement at Sydney Cove on 26 January 1788;
    b) Aborigines and Torres Strait Islanders suffered dispossession and dispersal upon acquisition of their traditional lands by the British Crown; and
    c) Aborigines and Torres Strait Islanders were denied full citizenship rights of the Commonwealth of Australia prior to the 1967 Referendum;
2 affirms:
    a) the importance of Aboriginal and Torres Strait Islander culture and heritage; and
    b) the entitlement of Aborigines and Torres Strait Islanders to self-management and self-determination subject to the Constitution and the laws of the Commonwealth of Australia; and

3 considers it desirable that the Commonwealth further promote
reconciliation with Aboriginal and Torres Strait Islander citizens
providing recognition of their special place in the Commonwealth of Australia.[4]

The Shadow Cabinet had decided it would support the
resolution only if the entitlement to self-determination
already qualified by the words 'subject to the Constitution
and the laws of the Commonwealth' were further qualified
by the words 'in common with all other Australians'. At best,
the proposed amendment was ambiguous suggesting that
the entitlement to self-determination was universal but
exercisable discretely by separate groups. At worst, it was
ruthlessly assimilationist; it suggested that self-determination could be exercised only collectively by all Australians
thereby excluding the Aboriginal choice between a
traditional lifestyle and the lifestyle of other Australians.

The Opposition's strong objection to the word 'self-
determination' was novel. Mr Miles, in reply to the Government's 'Foundations for the Future' statement the previous
December, had told Parliament:

In regard to self-determination, we accept the Government's aim
that Aboriginal and Islander people should be properly involved
in the decision-making process in order that the right decisions
are made about their lives. . . . Secondly, self-determination must
lead to self-sufficiency.[5]

During the debate on the resolution, Mr Howard said:
'Bipartisanship is not an end in itself; bipartisanship makes
sense only if we are bipartisan about the right policy.'[6] The
cost of bipartisanship would have been a resolution
unacceptable to the Aboriginal leadership. The resolution
would have been so weak that it would not have affirmed
the sole rationale for special laws and measures for
Aborigines. Unlike Vietnamese refugees or English migrants
in Australia, Aborigines have, for good reason, recently been

granted inalienable title to land and Aboriginal courts have been set up and been empowered to take account of local usages and customs in Aboriginal communities. The Aboriginal entitlement to self-determination must go beyond that which is enjoyed in common with all other Australians. Whatever scope the term 'self-determination' may develop in international law, that entitlement stood restrictively qualified in the resolution.

The only appeal of the amendment was to those who were party to the 'One Australia' debate in the joint party room of the Opposition. Though some Opposition members attempted to put forward more reasoned arguments for the amendment, the emotional appeals to 'One Australia' carried over from the migration debate were the determining factors. Ian Sinclair, Leader of the National Party, mentioned 'One Australia' five times during his short speech.

The entitlement of Aborigines and Torres Strait Islanders to self-management and self-determination, subject to the constitution and laws of the Commonwealth of Australia, does not entail any separate philosophy of a nation within a nation. Rather it affirms the entitlement of indigenous peoples to choose freely between their traditional lifestyles and that of other Australians. Although this choice is not, in the same sense, open to or made by other Australians, it is a necessary choice for indigenous people retaining a special affinity, as they do, with their land and trying to adapt across cultures to a harmonious co-existence with the new settlers and their descendants.

The Opposition was locked into its 'One Australia' policy and rhetoric, which stated that loyalty to Australian institutions and values should transcend loyalty to any other sets of values anywhere in the world. But even this rhetoric does not preclude loyalty to Aboriginal institutions and Aboriginal values. Justice and tolerance demand recognition of these, although they differ from mainstream Australian values and institutions. Aboriginal values and institutions may be unfamiliar to most Australians but they are definitely not alien.

Defending the Government against Opposition claims that the motion was 'purely symbolic and therefore of no importance or relevance to the Aboriginal and Islander people',[7] the Prime Minister quoted Dr (Nugget) Coombs, who with poet Judith Wright established the Aboriginal Treaty Committee:

It is never divisive to correct injustice. The fact of injustice is divisive and will continue to be until we correct it and learn to live with it. People who benefit from injustice will oppose this, but you don't stop working for justice simply because people around you don't like it.[8]

In the Senate debate, Aboriginal Anglican Bishop Arthur Malcolm was quoted:

Deep down, the majority of Aboriginal people long to hear at Government level an apology and admission that this was the Aboriginal peoples' land, that they are its forefathers and that white Australia is sorry that this was not recognised and acknowledged from the start. Until this happens, I don't see much headway coming – it has to be a two-way action.[9]

The withdrawal of Opposition support for the resolution cheated Parliament of one of the rare opportunities for finding what previous Liberal ministers have described as the 'common ground for negotiating a just settlement in both social and economical terms with Australia's Aboriginal people'.[10]

On 20 October 1988, the final report of the Constitutional Commission was tabled in the Parliament. The commission was chaired by Sir Maurice Byers QC, former Solicitor-General for the Commonwealth. The other members included two professors of law, a former Liberal State Premier and former Prime Minister, Gough Whitlam. The

commission had received a report from an Advisory
Committee on the Distribution of Powers chaired by Sir
John Moore and including a retired State Labor Premier,
Don Dunstan, who had been instrumental in introducing
land rights in his home state. In its consideration of the
treaty issue the committee expressed 'uneasiness about the
lack of an adequate public response especially from persons
representing the wide and diverse groups of Australian
Aborigines'.[11] It advised against seeking a referendum to
provide the necessary framework for a compact, having
examined the 1983 Senate report and found that there had
not been any radical change or real development in people's
thinking about the compact since then. The committee
quoted the Northern Land Council's submission in its
report:

Neither concept of makarrata or treaty enjoyed the full support
of the Aboriginal and Islander peoples. It is however recognised
by the Northern Land Council that at some time in the future it
may be generally thought desirable by Aboriginal and Islander
people to enter one or several agreements with the Commonwealth.[12]

There being no agreement between the Commonwealth
and the Aboriginal community on the compact's desirability, the committee concluded that there was a need for
'a greater indication of support for the general concept ...
before it becomes desirable to seek an amendment of the
Constitution for this purpose'.[13] The committee thought the
consultative process 'could take many years, especially
given the fact that traditionally the Aboriginal peoples'
decision-making processes are very slow and that it is
important that they should be allowed to reach consensus
on the matter by means of their own choosing'.[14]

Addressing the content of the parliamentary resolution
of 23 August 1988, the commission had no doubt that the

Commonwealth had sufficient constitutional power to take appropriate action to assist in the promotion of reconciliation with Aborigines and Torres Strait Islander citizens and to recognise their special place in the Commonwealth of Australia. The commission did not want to decide if an agreement (or number of agreements) was an appropriate path to reconciliation, and advised against the course proposed by the 1983 Senate Committee of Constitutional Amendment prior to the negotiation of an agreement.

At the end of 1988 Mr Hawke described the treaty as 'an umbrella document providing direction and perspective to all areas of policy', 'a reciprocal statement of obligation and reconciliation between the first occupants of Australia and those who have arrived since 1788'. It would be 'negotiated by people who share one nation and the one future – it will be a treaty between Australians and for Australians'.[15] Mr Howard said that a treaty 'must inevitably lead to claims for national land rights and massive compensation'. He saw a treaty as 'a recipe for separatism' that 'would not result in the development of compassionate and sensible policies so desperately needed to overcome the situation faced by many Aboriginal people'.[16]

Mr Yunupingu responded to the Coalition's 'One Australia' rhetoric agreeing that 'there should be one Australia and we should be part of it. But our part should be on our terms'.[17] Another Aborigine, Bob Liddle, opposed a treaty because 'Aborigines played a part in developing Australia. Aboriginal troopers and soldiers defended it. They want to share in Australia's future – not contest it'.[18]

The ambiguities of 1988 showed there was still unfinished business from the year's celebrations. The glitter of the national party did not completely distract the nation from the black history of white Australia. Many Australians saw for the first time that there was an Aboriginal perspective to the past 200 years. The bicentennial theme of 'Living Together' was neither an accurate expression of Aboriginal history nor of Aboriginal lives.

Looking to the next big date on the national calender, 1 January 2001, the first centenary of our federation, we need to do more so that even Aborigines might be proud to proclaim that we are 'living together' in this land.

From Treaty to Instrument of Reconciliation

The Aboriginal Peoples and Treaties conference, held at the University of New South Wales on 11 February 1989, provided the first opportunity for Aboriginal leaders and academic lawyers to come together and discuss the treaty proposal since the 1983 Aborigines and International Law conference. Mr Michael Mansell, an Aboriginal barrister from Tasmania, was as ever a forthright presence. Having been welcomed in Libya and been refused admission to Parliament House in Canberra for an official Government reception during the bicentenary, he knows he is not well accommodated in the mainstream of Australian party politics. He gave an analysis of the four options proposed by the 1983 Senate Committee report and demonstrated that all these options were based on the assumption that 'Aborigines are Australian citizens and ought to be'.[19]

Mansell cautioned against any of these options because each required an Aboriginal acceptance of 'the legitimacy of the invasion of this country'. He thought that would sell short Aboriginal claims. As Australian Aborigines rather than Aboriginal Australians he argued for the recognition of indigenous rights that flow from that separate identity, rather than the concession of rights by the colonising Government. Whatever the niceties of the philosophical differences between the major political parties, Mansell accused the Prime Minister and the Leader of the Opposition of jumping into the same bed whenever the question of Aboriginal statehood arose and proclaiming with one voice: 'We are all Australians'. He laid down the challenge to the Aborigines present: 'If we are not part of the Australian nation but a separate nation of people unto ourselves, then we have to get our act together.'

If Mansell's remarks did reflect the view of a significant number of Aborigines, he was highlighting the chasm that exists in understanding about the whole nature of Mr Hawke's enterprise. Nothing Hawke nor his ministers has ever said has given grounds for presuming that separate nationhood is on the agenda. Treaty talk once again was put on the Canberra back-burner as the Government became embroiled in the saga of consultation and legislation for the new Aboriginal and Torres Strait Islander Commission.

When the Hawke Government introduced the system of super-departments in the Commonwealth public service, the Department of Aboriginal Affairs (DAA) had been undergoing a process of Aboriginalisation. All positions in the department were identified as requiring an ability to communicate with Aborigines and/or a knowledge of Aboriginal culture. In practice this meant that Aborigines were more likely to be employed as public servants. Rather than amalgamating the DAA with other departments (which did not have a policy of Aboriginalisation), Mr Hawke promised to set up an Aboriginal commission to replace the department. As a statutory commission, ATSIC was structured so as to provide Aborigines with even more control over the administration of government programmes, though subject to strict financial accountability.

The ATSIC legislation had a very troubled passage. It took over two years and the final Bill was debated in the Senate for forty hours and amended more than one hundred times. On 5 March 1990, five interim commissioners nominated by the Minister, Gerry Hand, took office for a year. Lois O'Donoghue, the first chairperson, referred to ATSIC as the 'voice of Australia's Aboriginal and Torres Strait Islander people'. She saw the commencement of ATSIC as the beginning of 'a unique and productive partnership with the Government'. Given the messiness of the consultation process and the public disinterest in the long parliamentary debate that resulted in many changes to the legislation, she was presumably including Aborigines as well as other Australians when she said: 'We have to overcome the pessimism and the scepticism of those with little faith or limited understanding about the aspirations and needs of Aboriginal Australians.' If ATSIC is to become the voice of Aboriginal Australia, it has much to do to win that accolade.

While at the Treaty of Waitangi celebrations in New Zealand in February 1990, Mr Hawke referred to treaty consultations and negotiations in Australia. At a news conference in Auckland he argued that 'via ATSIC' the Government would 'have a better way of getting the views of the Aboriginal community'.[20] Predictably this drew a strong response from Geoff Clarke, the Co-ordinator of the National Federation of Land Councils, who said that ATSIC's function was to administer government services not to negotiate a treaty. He excluded even the primary use of the ATSIC structure for consultations, saying: 'Nor should ATSIC fund treaty discussions. A Treaty Commission needs to be completely separate. It should be funded from a special appropriation similar to Royal Commissions'.[21] There are many Aboriginal organisations throughout the country that pride themselves on being more independent from government and more accountable to their local constituencies than a national newcomer like ATSIC, which chiefly administers government funds with full accountability to Government. Though ATSIC may come to be seen as a representative body for Aborigines, it will not do so while many of the acknowledged Aboriginal leaders are out of it and mistrustful of Government processes. The Government's handling of the Aboriginal Development Commission (ADC) in its last days ensured that even some of the more moderate Aboriginal leaders would treat the ATSIC structure with considerable suspicion.

In response to the 1989 parliamentary purge of Aboriginal

affairs, Aboriginal supporters in the Hawke Government had found themselves with no option but to tighten up on accountability. No one in the Opposition begged to differ. Clipping the wings of the ADC, which had been set up by the Fraser Government, Mr Hawke said his Government, like its predecessors, had been prepared in the past to accept an element of risk in allowing the ADC to operate 'with a less than conventional level of ministerial oversight for a statutory authority'.[22] But the picnic was over. In May 1989 Mr Hand told the Parliament: 'We have made changes to the original concept and the question of accountability is one of the main ones. That is the trade off for participation.'[23] To the irritation of the heavily scrutinised community councils under state jurisdiction, Hand claimed: 'There is no other department or statutory authority in existence in the Commonwealth which will be as accountable as ATSIC,' and went on to defy the Opposition to find him 'any organisation under this Government or any other Government that will be as accountable as this structure'.[24]

Despite such tight Government scrutiny of ATSIC finances, the commission has broad powers and great potential. Funds can be allocated to a housing fund and to the Regional Land Fund for the purchase of land on the open market in accordance with the wishes of regional councils. Consultants can be employed and advisory committees set up. The Prime Minister can confer other departmental functions on the commission and the States can confer their functions on the commission if the Minister approves.

In Parliament, much attention was given to a lengthy preamble to the ATSIC legislation, which espoused many lofty sentiments about Aboriginal history and aspirations. This preamble was ultimately dropped altogether from the legislation. Though it referred to Aborigines and Torres Strait Islanders as being 'the prior occupiers and original owners of this land', it went on to assert that they 'have no recognised rights over land other than those granted or recognised by the Crown'. Earlier versions were even more restrictive in the 'recognition' of Aboriginal rights. Before being discarded by the Senate, the preamble went through the House of Representatives twice and in each second reading speech Mr Hand said it was intended to have no legal effect:

The Government's intention has . . . always been that the language of the preamble would be neutral and have no legal consequences for present or future litigation in relation to land claims. The language was, and is, in no way intended to recognise land rights claimed to exist, to create new rights for land or compensation or to remove or qualify rights under existing law. Nor was it, or is it, intended to restrict any future developments in the law.

When endorsed by the Parliament in the name of the Australian people, the Preamble will stand as an historical expression of philosophy and principle. The intention that the Preamble has no legal consequences in no way detracts from its importance as a statement of those facts. I am happy to state that the Preamble has the support not only of the vast majority of the indigenous groups of this nation but also will, I am confident, enjoy the support of the wider community throughout Australia.[25]

Both parties played a cat and mouse game about the legal consequences of the preamble. The Opposition was concerned that an admission of prior Aboriginal ownership might give rise to claims for compensation for past dispossession. Mr Hand told Parliament that he had 'received no specific advice of a legal nature on that point'.[26] Later the Attorney-General did confirm that legal advice had been obtained from his department in the form of the usual co-ordination comment that accompanies Cabinet submissions. Also the Government had received oral advice from a QC who was arguing a land rights case for the Commonwealth in the High Court at the time. But the Government refused to make public either advice, thereby contributing to public disquiet about the legal effect of the preamble. It was not the way to gain bipartisan support. The Coalition wanted to avoid the developments in New Zealand, which had come about through the failure of both Government and the Opposition to predict that the Treaty of Waitangi would become 'a living document' as the result of a piece of legislation regarding state incorporations. The Hawke Government wanted the Howard Opposition to sign a blank cheque.

The Government's failure to release the legal advice meant the preamble was doomed because Democrats in the Senate saw it as dishonest. The preamble did not relate to the content of the ATSIC Bill. Ultimately, the Government was forced to take up a suggestion of the Democrats that the words of the preamble be passed in the Senate as a separate resolution committing the Parliament to the negotiation of a charter of reconciliation.

Rhetorical preambles have become very popular in Commonwealth legislation dealing with Aborigines. Usually a preamble has no legal effect; it simply expresses the purpose or sentiment of the legislation that follows. In 1987 the Hawke Government had introduced two Bills to Parliament at the request of the Cain Government in Victoria that was having difficulty convincing a hostile Upper House to pass its own legislation.[27] In these preambles the Government of Victoria acknowledged the occupation of Victoria by the Aboriginal people before the arrival of Europeans, and the importance to the Aboriginal people and to the wider community of the Aboriginal culture and heritage. It also acknowledged that the land in question was traditionally owned, occupied, used and enjoyed by Aborigines in accordance with Aboriginal laws, customs, traditions and practices and that the land had been taken by force from the local clan without consideration as to compensation under common law or without regard to Aboriginal law.

The Commonwealth Parliament passed each of these Acts in haste before it rose for the 1987 election. However, for the first time in the history of the federation it inserted a disclaimer that 'the Commonwealth does not acknowledge the matters acknowledged by the Government of Victoria'. In passing this legislation at the request of the Government of Victoria, the Commonwealth Parliament could have remained silent. But on advice from the Attorney-General's Department and from counsel acting for the Commonwealth in land rights matters, these specific words of disclaimer were inserted. Even after the passing of the ATSIC legislation, which amended these two earlier Acts, the Government refused to remove its offensive repudiation. In distancing itself from the Victorian acknowledgements, the Commonwealth provided a clear indication of the parameters within which it is prepared to negotiate an agreement.

The failure to amend when there was an opportunity without cost or inconvenience, set the parameters in concrete. The history of these preambles highlights the Commonwealth Government's uncertain and slipshod commitment to finding a consistent legislative formula that could express Aboriginal entitlements. It provides no grounds for presuming that the treaty process will result in individual or collective rights being created or recognised, made enforceable by law and enjoyed on the basis of race.

Senator Michael Tate had the carriage of the ATSIC Bill in the Senate. The debate on the preamble further clarified the Government's position. Though there may have been a commitment to an Aboriginal-driven consultation process, it was not as if Aborigines had a free hand. In particular, it was made even clearer than Mr Holding had done in 1983, that sovereignty was non-negotiable. Not even by the words of a resolution or preamble was there to be any room for suspicion that independent sovereign status was being accorded to or even being entertained for Aborigines. Tate, who was by then the Minister for Justice and who had chaired the Senate committee that produced the 1983 report on the makarrata, was emphatic:

It cannot be said often enough that that indissoluble Commonwealth has but one sovereignty, and that is expressed in this Parliament by the elected representatives of the Australian people. That paramount sovereignty which resides here is recognised in a sense in the making of a resolution of the Parliament dealing with these matters or to putting in a preamble to an enactment of the Parliament. Nothing in the statute before us or, I believe, in the wording of the resolution that Senator Coulter has put to this chamber, intentionally or inadvertently creates a situation of dual sovereignty, apartheid or separatism.[28]

As if that were not enough, he continued:

I do not believe that any Australian would tolerate for one moment the creation of a situation by resolution, preamble or, certainly, enactment, in which dual sovereignty was allowed to creep into our society. There is but one nation, one indissoluble Commonwealth, in which all peoples of Australia are united.[29]

In the Senate, the Democrats had proposed a resolution that repeated the numerous acknowledgements in the original preamble of the ATSIC Bill.[30] The Democrats' resolution included acknowledgements that no serious attempt was made to reach a lasting and equitable agreement with Aborigines on the use of their land, and that it was the wish of the people of Australia that a real and lasting reconciliation be reached with the Aboriginal and Torres Strait Islander peoples. The resolution embraced the aims of self-determination and self-management for the Aboriginal and Torres Strait Islander peoples within the Australian nation.

The resolution also declared 'that an instrument of understanding and reconciliation with the Aboriginal and Torres Strait Islander peoples should be negotiated by the Australian Government'. The resolution was carried in the Senate with support from the Government two months after it had been placed on the notice paper. The understanding was that it would be proposed by the Government in the House of Representatives. Senator John Coulter, the Democrat Spokesperson on Aboriginal Affairs, had closed his remarks in the mammoth Senate session with a plea to the Prime Minister:

a motion dealing with this matter was moved by the Prime Minister in the House of Representatives on the first day of sitting in this new Parliament House, and it would be very appropriate, when this resolution goes down to the House of Representatives, that it be put to the House not by the Minister for Aboriginal Affairs, Gerry Hand, but by the Prime Minister of Australia. That would elevate it to the importance that it should have.[31]

His plea went unheeded. Despite the fact that the Government had agreed in the Senate to the preamble being removed from the Bill and duly voted for it as a separate motion, the Prime Minister told the Democrats that he would not proceed with the resolution in the lower house because the impact of the preamble had been lessened by its separation from the legislation to which it bore no relation anyway. He wrote 'that no repetition of replacement resolutions will overcome that loss of impact'.[32] In the end, the House of Representatives passed neither the preamble nor the resolution. Self-determination, the treaty proposal, and even the modest suggestion of an instrument of understanding and reconciliation, once again went on to the back-burner.

During debate on the Democrat resolution, Senator Chris Puplick, who enjoyed a reputation in the Liberal Party for his progressive views on social issues, took over from Senator Peter Baume and led the debate for the Coalition. He said that such an instrument was 'something which had previously been referrred to as a makarrata, a treaty or a compact. It has been through all sorts of manifestations and we have opposed it in all of them'. In earlier days as Minister, Baume had actually assisted the development of the makarrata idea and congratulated Aborigines for the use of the term. For the Coalition, Puplick was spelling an unambiguous end to all bipartisanship saying:

I can think of nothing more divisive, nothing more fundamentally likely to increase tensions and divisions or to set group against group, person against person, institution against institution, than a motion passed by the Commonwealth Parliament which says that we want to have an instrument of understanding and reconciliation.[33]

Mr Hawke continued to restate his total commitment to the concept of a treaty. On 31 July 1989, Cabinet had called for a submission 'outlining the strategy for developing the treaty or compact'. But as will be seen in the next chapter, the Department of Foreign Affairs had been putting a different complexion on things overseas. The Australian Government had been making substantive contributions to the review of Convention 107 of the International Labour Organisation (ILO) and to the development by the Working Group on Indigenous Populations (WGIP) of the draft Declaration of Indigenous Rights. Australia had been represented at all sessions of the WGIP. After the seventh session in 1989, the Australian Government ruled out any possibility of compensation for lands already alienated and cautioned against the use of the word 'treaty' in referring to domestic arrangements with indigenous populations.

With the ATSIC legislation passed, Mr Hawke thought his minister, Mr Hand, would have more time to dedicate to the treaty consultations, negotiations and education processes. He hoped to see real progress during 1990 out of which would emerge a treaty 'which is meaningful and will represent a recognition by non-Aboriginal Australians of the injustices of the past. And reciprocally a recognition from the Aboriginal and Torres Strait Island communities that that is a meaningful recognition by non-Aboriginal Australians'.[34]

At the Treaty of Waitangi celebrations in February 1990, Mr Hawke gave the assurance that the consultation and negotiation of the treaty would be processed in the Government's fourth term, and that 'the resources will be made available because I do believe that the total Australian community ... is going to be well served by the achievement of that treaty'.[35] During the 1990 election campaign a month later, the ALP said that consultations on a treaty had been delayed by problems in establishing ATSIC and by the time taken to refute the allegations of Aboriginal mismanagement made in Senate Estimates Committees. On the campaign trail, Hawke repeated his hope that ATSIC would provide a means for collecting the views of Aborigines on the treaty. He hoped to process the treaty in the life of the new Parliament.[36]

The National Federation of Land Councils meeting in the Gariwerd National Park, was not impressed. Their members called for the establishment of a treaty commission independently funded and with UN involvement. The Coalition parties continued with their unco-operative approach during the 1990 election campaign. The Liberals said the proposal for a treaty was flawed in legal, political and historical terms.[37] The Nationals said a treaty was potentially divisive and meaningless. They presumptuously asserted that 'the majority of Aborigines do not want any so-called treaty'.[38] These Opposition statements offered little hope of change through the national parliamentary processes. During a campaign interview Mr Peacock, then Leader of the Opposition, continued his predecessor's 'One Australia' rhetoric:

I don't understand, as a lawyer, how you can have a treaty with yourself. I start with the proposition that I believe in us all working for a united Australia, all people being joined together under one flag, under the rule of law operating as one nation: a whole multiplicity of backgrounds, of colour, of creed. Now if that is the case, how do you serve the purpose of a united community by suddenly embarking on a treaty within that country?[39]

Meanwhile at least one high-profile Aborigine had come to see the years of treaty talk and argument by politicians as a distraction from the real issues. Gary Foley was quoted the day before the election saying that the treaty was not an idea that had emanated from Aborigines:

We don't know of any treaty in the world that has worked effectively for the weaker party. The first and foremost issue is land rights and economic independence. The more cynical among us may be inclined to suggest that the talk of a treaty is designed to defuse the real issue.[40]

After winning a record fourth term, Mr Hawke wrote to Dr Hewson, the new Leader of the Opposition, advising him 'of the Government's wish to achieve a more bipartisan approach in furthering the welfare of the Aborigines and Torres Strait Islanders and advancing the concept of an instrument of reconciliation'.[41] Hewson responded to Hawke six weeks later. Treating Hawke's letter as a 'sounding out' of the Coalition's support for a process of reconciliation, he replied:

I would point out, as stated specifically in our current policy, that the Coalition 'is open to consideration of proposals which will improve relationships between Aborigines and other Australians'. It is not possible, however, to give any firm commitment to a more bipartisan approach to a process of reconciliation at this stage until we know precisely what it is you intend to propose.
 You acknowledge that the Coalition recognises the importance of reconciliation and, to this end, we would like to know how you intend to proceed with regards to a process of reconciliation as there may be room for considerable common ground.[42]

Hawke had paid tribute to the Coalition's achievements

when in government for the betterment of Aborigines, including the 1967 referendum, the Bonner resolution, the NAC–Government discussions on the makarrata, the Aboriginal Development Commission, and the 1983 Senate Committee report. He could also have included the Land Rights Act for the Northern Territory. He noted that all these measures 'received strong bipartisan support'. Pleading for a return to bipartisanship, he claimed broad agreement between the parties on some objectives including Aboriginal self-sufficiency, improvement in health, education, employment and housing.

Hewson welcomed the call to bipartisanship as a significant break with the recent past. He claimed that the bipartisan approach had been broken in the past seven years by the 'Government's pursuit of the National Land Rights legislation, your Treaty proposal and ATSIC'. By this time, even the elder statesman of the Liberal Party, Fred Chaney, who maintained a watchful eye on Aboriginal Affairs, was exasperated with the Labor Government's approach. He accused the ALP of having applied itself 'to romance, to theory, to totems and to self-indulgence'.[43] Critical of insufficiently monitored programmes, duplication of services and administrative inefficiencies, Hewson was sure that Hawke would understand 'that we would not want a more bipartisan approach to limit us from criticising your Government so long as we perceive these issues as being inadequately addressed'. Many members of the Coalition were of the view that the Government only sought bipartisanship in Aboriginal Affairs when it was in trouble. They were not about to let the Government off the hook, whatever the commitment to reconciliation.

Seeking to avoid the semantic debate about the word 'treaty' Hawke stressed his belief that:

The consultation processes will be as important as the eventual outcome. But there is little hope of a worthwhile outcome, even to consultations, without the support of the majority of Australians.

I understand that in the recent past the Coalition, on the basis of an assumption that the nature of a 'treaty' involves an agreement between two nations, has stated its opposition to such a cause. I assure you that it has never been in the Government's mind that the reconciliation process lead to such an outcome.

Nothing could be clearer, despite the reservations of some Aboriginal leaders. The instrument, whatever it might be called, is to have no implications whatever in international law. Despite this, Hewson restated the objections to a treaty or anything like it:

Our opposition to a treaty is based on our strongly held belief that Australians belong to one nation and one group of Australians cannot have a treaty with the rest of the nation.

It has been our consistent position since 1981 that a treaty has implications in international law which are unacceptable to the Australian people.

Whatever Hewson was opposing, it was not what Hawke was proposing, nor what he has ever proposed. If the Opposition were to reject Hawke's proposal, they would have to admit their position was now inconsistent with what they had proposed, or at least tolerated, in 1981, namely a negotiated agreement with Aborigines subject to constraints and having no effect in international law.

As Leader of the Opposition, Peacock had criticised the Government for its resort to highly symbolic gestures in place of the administration of effective programmes. This false dichotomy between the symbolic and the material overlooked the possibility that there was a need for effecive programmes as well as symbolic gestures. Without effective programmes, symbolic gestures will be a sham anyway. Hewson has continued to speak in terms of a dichotomy:

In our view, an ongoing process of reconciliation and adequate positive programs and material support which leads to a significant improvement in the standard of living, quality of life and self esteem of Aboriginal Australians would enhance their cause in a more meaningful way than a treaty or similar instrument.[44]

There is no reason why there should not be both a process and an instrument of reconciliation. Hewson recognised 'the importance of symbolism in Aboriginal culture' but made no reference to the importance of symbolism for all Australians in seeking to express our true identity, reconciled with our past. To date, the Coalition has seen no place for national symbolic action for reconciliation through parliamentary processes.

Reconciliation will not be furthered by harping on collective guilt for the past but it can be brought about by taking collective responsibility for our present social reality. In this our national politicians could have a role to play. During the 1989 ATSIC debate, Senator John Stone expressed his reservations, shared by many members of the Coalition, about the place of government in seeking national reconciliation. Rodney Rivers, an Aborigine from Toowoomba, had written a letter to the *Australian*. He told the story of his grandmother who had been separated in the 1930s from her husband, 'rounded up by police on horseback at Landsdowne station and made to walk to Fitzroy Crossing in chains with her sister for about three days over rough terrain'. Mr Rivers wrote:

We do not hold or harbour grudges or ill-feelings towards those who treated us unkindly in the past. They are forgiven. Certainly, we cannot condone what happened in the past – but neither can we condemn the innocent white race of today and try to force them to pay restitution for events they played no part in.

We of today are responsible for the present and the future, not for the past. He or she who does not forgive breaks the bridge over which they, too, someday have to cross; for each one of us needs to be forgiven![45]

Senator Stone paid a moving tribute in Parliament to Mr Rivers (who, as it turned out, was active in the Logos Foundation, which was supporting the National Party in the Queensland election campaign):

That gentleman has done us a great service by writing that letter and putting on record not only the wrongs that were done to his family but also the manner in which he has approached the historical burden, if you like, which those wrongs placed on him.[46]

That historical burden has been placed on all Australians who now seek to live together in harmony in this land. Senator Stone drew a lesson from the letter: 'that government had nothing to do with that gentleman's reconciliation and coming to terms with his fellow Australians'. Over a long period in the public service, he had 'not noticed governments do much good in matters of this kind'. But even if it be conceded that governments do not achieve much in this regard, it is another question whether or not the sovereign Parliament of Australia, the people's parliament, has any role to play, not in assuaging collective guilt but in expressing collective responsibility and effecting understanding and reconciliation. It should be possible for our Parliament to speak with one voice on the need for understanding and reconciliation. If not, it is continuing evidence that we are a divided nation, divided by our history. This is not to argue that reconciliation is the sole or primary domain of politicians, but they do have a role in shaping laws and policies that complement the reconciliation that people like Mr Rivers have been able to effect.

Dr Hewson says the Opposition 'remains to be convinced that an instrument of reconciliation would provide any lasting tangible benefit to Aboriginal people'. Others remain to be convinced that we can continue to do without it. If the Opposition is prepared to support an instrument that is likely to produce tangible results, presumably there is scope for bipartisan support of an instrument having some teeth, rather than one that is purely symbolic.

It was inevitable that the Hawke Government's attempts to seek bipartisan support through processes that honoured the procedures of party rooms and shadow cabinet, would create an impression among some Aboriginal leaders that the Government and Opposition were discussing Aboriginal issues in quarantine. Terry O'Shane, while an interim ATSIC commissioner, pointed to the need for three-way discussions involving the Government, the Opposition and Aboriginal leaders, and that 'land rights and treaty will be on the agenda'.[47]

Lois O'Donoghue, Chairperson of ATSIC, wants the term 'treaty' retained and sees ATSIC playing a central role in negotiations. The Opposition has made it clear that the term is unacceptable and the Government has conceded this as the price to be paid for bipartisanship.[48] This has led Michael Mansell and others to announce moves for the creation of a provisional government for Aborigines committed to the formation of an independent Aboriginal state situated on lands in the centre of Australia. He and his self-appointed ministers are not traditional owners of that area. Neither have the traditional owners sought nor approved the provisional government. According to Mr Mansell, the common thread of this Aboriginal Utopia will weave through every corner of the continent:

The boundaries of areas of the Aboriginal nation will be as diverse and unspectacular as are the boundaries of some other countries of the world. Initially small Aboriginal communities seeking independence will lead the way for others. The common purpose of independence from the harshness of white control will be the thread joining up these smaller Aboriginal groups until eventually, even if still separated geographically, they constitute an

Aboriginal nation capable of controlling itself without interference, raising its own economies, making and enforcing its laws
and deciding its own future.[49]

Asked about applying for Federal Government funding
assistance, he said: 'We would not take money from a
government we're opposed to.'[50] No process or instrument
of reconciliation will satisfy him and his supporters. Those
who espouse it will be identified as 'the good old reac-
tionaries who sit in their homes being experts on Aboriginal
affairs and who denounce any radical initiative as having
the potential to put the Aboriginal cause back ten years'.[51]

Meanwhile the Hawke initiative drew a positive response
and assurance of co-operation from the Queensland
National Party. Their leader, Russell Cooper, thinks 'all Australians can benefit from such an approach with the end
result being an increased national pride'.[52] It would be
strange and regrettable and there would be grounds for
suspicion, if the quest for bipartisanship were to result in
widespread Aboriginal disillusionment and complete
satisfaction from the Queensland National Party.

Despite the Hawke Government's desire to avoid the
term 'treaty', the ATSIC commissioners have refused to
concede, whatever the sensibilities of the Federal Opposition. They have resolved to pursue what Lois O'Donoghue
described to the National Immigration Outlook Conference
in November 1990 as an act of reconciliation that 'would
help heal old wounds, acknowledge the rightful place of
indigenous people in this nation and provide a just basis
for the new society which Aboriginal people and the new
arrivals are building in this continent'.[53]

Robert Tickner has been a strong advocate for the
bipartisan approach. Speaking in Geneva in August 1990,
he claimed there were 'some wonderful signs of hope that
Government and Opposition may be able to work together
to promote a process of reconciliation'. Aware that reconciliation talk can be shallow unless it is backed by adequate

programmes, he has set as a precondition: 'the adoption of a national goal for all levels of government working with Aboriginal people to address co-operatively issues of land, housing, health infrastructure, education, employment and economic development of Aboriginal Australia in the period leading up to the centenary of federation in 2001'.[54] Unfortunately his sweeping agenda did not rate a mention in the Prime Minister's address on constitutional review at the National Press Club the previous month. There Hawke set down an 'achievable, yet wide-ranging agenda for change and reform' before convening a Special Premiers' Conference to plan reform until 2001. Unless it comes on to the agenda at premiers' conferences the instrument of reconciliation is a long way from being an achievable constitutional reform and it will remain a Canberra abstraction. Aborigines will be left with the empty consolation that the process is more important than the outcome.

In the 1991 Budget, the Government provided $3 million for the reconciliation process. Administered by a task force in the Department of Prime Minister and Cabinet, this process has some chance of being tied to the general process of constitutional review. Competent Aboriginal administrators like Pat Turner and Dawn Casey may be able to give the process life and legitimacy. In December 1990, Cabinet endorsed Tickner's discussion paper on Aboriginal reconciliation, and a Council of Aboriginal Reconciliation is to be established by an Act of Parliament. It will exist until 1 January 2001 and of the twenty-five members, about half will be Aboriginal. The Government will then be distanced from the process of reconciliation. It is important that the Council not be seen to be effecting or delivering reconciliation from on high. Council initiatives and efforts of individual councillors should be a catalyst for reconciliation in local communities throughout Australia. Hopefully, the review of legal recognition and protection of Aboriginal entitlements to self-management and self-determination will become an integral part of the review of the constitutional basis of our federation in the next decade.

Then, provided we have a formula of words that expresses the place of Aborigines in Australian society, we might achieve the dream of Galarrwuy Yunupingu, the elder from the North who signed the Barunga Statement with the Prime Minister in 1988:

What we want from a treaty is the creation of a just and mature society which black and white Australians can enjoy together. A treaty which recognises our rights and our status will provide the basis for building a society in which people live in mutual respect. To those people who say they support the concept of 'One Australia' I can only say that I agree. There should be one Australia and we should be part of it. But our part should be on our terms.

A treaty will wipe out injustice and redress the wrongs of today, which can be traced to the wrongs of the past. It will put us on the right track for the future. It will create an Australia we can all share in pride. It will mean, in 2088 and 2188 and all the other '88's, ALL Australians celebrating their achievement.[55]

These unexceptionable sentiments should not be rail-roaded simply by semantic debate over terms like treaty and self-determination. There are real differences between Yunipingu's approach and that of Mansell and his Aboriginal Provisional Government. It is time to look at the substance of those differences, to assess their acceptance in Aboriginal communities and to debate their justification. Any view that commands acceptance and justification deserves a run on the national political agenda.

FOUR:

THE CLOUDS OF GENEVA

In 1492 Europeans and Indians discovered each other and to each there opened a new world. For centuries Christopher Columbus has been described as the discoverer and the Indians as the discovered. 1992 is the 500th anniversary of Columbus's achievement. The UN is to mark the following year as the International Year of the World Indigenous Peoples.

Indigenous people have become increasingly active in taking their struggle on to the international stage. Their claims to land rights, sovereignty and self-determination are being heard in international fora, where they hope that the restrictive notions of private property, national sovereignty and assimilation will not enjoy the same currency as they do in their domestic political situation.

After the Second World War, the UN committed itself to the decolonisation process. Native peoples with an identifiable population and land base were entitled to self-determination. Local populations could make a free choice whether or not to be integrated into the adjacent society administered by the colonising power. When separated by blue water or by identifiable boundaries, such populations could decide to separate and seek their own development. During decolonisation, people were to be guaranteed a free choice in determining their new political status. Indigenous minorities within the boundaries of nation states started agitating for a similar free choice on the basis that they had never been consulted nor consented to their own colonisation.

Some Aboriginal leaders and their supporters have abandoned the Australian political process as a waste of time in the quest for guaranteed indigenous rights. Rather they entertain hopes that international initiatives, especially with agencies of the UN, will compel or at least shame the government back home into making meaningful concessions to their demands. Annual trips to Geneva are now a regular task for these leaders and their legal advisers. During the term of the Hawke Government, the usual venues have been the International Labour Organisation (ILO) and the UN Working Group on Indigenous Populations.

These international meetings have provided Aboriginal groups with new ideas and networks. But it is a mistake for Aborigines and their supporters to think that they will be able to bypass the negotiation process back home by gaining concessions in Geneva. Much of the international debate is bogged down in semantic discussion of terms that have to be so generally defined as to cover all conceivable situations. Wandering through the maze of UN initialised bodies, delegates to international conferences readily become convinced that the process is more important than the outcome. For indigenous people, however, there have been very few outcomes and few are to be expected. The past nine years of feverish activity have achieved no substantive agreement between governments and indigenous people. The annual meetings are little more than political word-games.

The UN Working Group on Indigenous Populations

In 1978 the UN held a world conference to combat racism and racial discrimination that dealt with indigenous people as part of its programme of action. The conference urged states to recognise the entitlement of indigenous people 'to carry on within their areas of settlement their traditional structure of economy and way of life' without affecting 'their right to participate freely on an equal basis in the economic, social and political development of the country'. The conference also encouraged the formation of international indigenous organisations that could participate in UN processes. Self-determination was on the agenda for indigenous minorities. Assimilation and integration were now seen as objectionable on the basis that they precluded freedom of choice.

In 1982 the Economic and Social Council of the United Nations (ECOSOC) approved a proposal for the establishment of a Working Group on Indigenous Populations (WGIP). In 1988, at the request of indigenous groups, the last word of the title was informally changed from 'populations' to 'peoples'. ECOSOC provided the working group with a mandate to review developments relating to the promotion and protection of the human rights of indigenous populations and to give special attention to the evolution of international standards. Since its establishment, the working group has met every year except 1986. It meets for at least five days in August before the annual meeting of the Sub-Commission on Prevention of Discrimination and Protection of Minorities. It is constituted by five members of the sub-commission who meet with indigenous representatives from a growing list of countries and then report to the sub-commission. The working group also makes its reports available to the UN Commission on Human Rights, which in turn has the power to make recommendations to ECOSOC.

The working group is drafting a universal declaration on the rights of indigenous peoples. In 1983 it received a report from one-time Mexican ambassador, Jose Martinez Cobo, who had been commissioned by the sub-commission in 1971 to make a study of discrimination against indigenous populations. He was convinced that 'self-determination, in its many forms, must be recognised as the basic precondition for the enjoyment of indigenous peoples of their fundamental rights and the determination of their own future'. But his concept of self-determination was very fluid. Though insisting that indigenous groups be assured freedom of choice, he did not see that choice as necessarily including the right to secede from the state in which they lived. He focussed not on sovereignty that would permit the group to choose separation, but on autonomy, which would permit the group to live differently, but within the one sovereign state.[1]

Aborigines and the Australian Government have played a significant role in the deliberations of the working group. After the first session the Australian Government made several suggestions about indigenous rights and sounded a warning that separate development for indigenous populations was not a choice open to them because they 'are an integral part of the national communities to which they belong and should enjoy the full civil and political rights of their fellow citizens, in addition to their own special rights'.[2] Content that its domestic policies would be consistent with any outcome that might result from the group's deliberations, the Government suggested that 'the right to pursue traditional lifestyles, special programmes to remedy dispossession, dispersal and disadvantage, and the principle of self-management' be reflected in any international standards being developed. The key issues were survival of indigenous populations, land rights and autonomy, not separate development or Aboriginal sovereignty.

In 1984 Clyde Holding, as Minister for Aboriginal Affairs, attended the working group and set out the Government's agenda for national land rights, which later miscarried. The Secretary of the Department of Aboriginal Affairs led the Government delegation in 1985, 1988 and 1989. Usually representatives from several Aboriginal organisations attend including the National Aboriginal and Islander Legal Service Secretariat (NAILSS), which has consultative status with ECOSOC, the National Aboriginal and Islander Health Organisation (NAIHO), the Federation of Land Councils,

the New South Wales Aboriginal Land Council and the
Tasmanian Aboriginal Centre. Lois O'Donoghue, the chairperson of ATSIC, addressed the working group in 1990 and
1991. Indigenous participants usually confer for a week or
two before meeting with the working group. Aboriginal
commitment to the process is strong and undoubtedly
expensive.

At the first few meetings, members of the working group
voiced their concerns that some indigenous spokespersons
were turning it into a chamber of complaints. In response,
the sub-commission resolved in 1984 that the working
group should 'relate its consideration of developments
affecting the rights of indigenous populations to the process
of preparing international standards'.[3]

Several Australian Aboriginal organisations are affiliated
with The World Council of Indigenous Peoples (WCIP), a
non-government organisation with consultative status to
UN bodies. It had prepared a draft declaration of the 'most
basic rights of indigenous peoples', which included the right
of self-determination, permitting free determination of
political status and economic, social, religious and cultural
development.[4]

Before the fourth session of the working group in 1985,
six non-government Aboriginal organisations (including
NAILSS) cobbled together a draft declaration of principles
that significantly expanded the WCIP draft. Both self-
determination and treaties were central concepts in this
draft. Self-determination entailed the right to choose whatever degree of autonomy or self-government was desired,
without external interference. Treaties and other agreements freely made with indigenous nations or peoples were
to be recognised and applied in the same manner and
according to the same international laws and principles as
treaties and agreements entered into with member states
of the UN.[5]

The working group found these concepts beyond the
pale, made no mention of self-determination nor treaties,

and restricted itself to unexceptionable principles expressed as formulations of individual and collective rights, including the rights to religious freedom, education in one's own language and preservation of cultural identity.

Even in these early stages, governments were making it clear that any declaration would be acceptable only if it fitted in with their various foreign policy agendas, none of which treats indigenous rights as central. Although the US was insisting on language that would include the Soviet Union's tribal peoples, the USSR was insisting that indigenous situations arise only in the Americas and Australasia where there are imported populations of Europeans. The Eastern Europeans were unhappy that the working group had moved from grievance hearing to standard-setting. Given that most indigenous delegations had come from the Americas, the old format maximised opportunities for embarrassing the West with no threat to the East. Standard-setting put both under scrutiny. The Indians and Chinese were insistent that there were no indigenous peoples in Asia, only minorities. India threatened to block any resolution unless it was limited expressly to the Americas, Australia and the Arctic regions.

Although the indigenous representatives at the 1985 meeting submitted a joint proposal on land rights, the working group simply annexed it to their report without comment. The various government observers were very reserved about collective political rights. For example, Norway put the modest guiding principle that indigenous peoples 'should have influence in the decision-making process concerning their own affairs'. Canada spoke of its commitment to 'establishing self-government structures at the local level', conceding that local indigenous control of public funds fell far short of self-determination. The agenda for the next meeting listed consideration of the right to autonomy, self-government and self-determination, including political representation and institutions.

In 1987 the indigenous people issued a draft of twenty-two principles for discussion and consultation. These principles were an expansion of the 1985 list. The emphasis on self-determination and treaties was maintained. For her part, the Chairperson of the working group, Professor Erica-Irene Daes, prepared a working paper of draft preliminary principles that was considered and rejected at the Indigenous Pre-Sessional Meeting in 1988. The seventy-five indigenous people at the meeting thought she had insufficient regard for the right of self-determination and the significance of treaties. She preferred to speak of 'autonomy'. Though the Soviet Union welcomed a draft that spoke of collective as well as individual rights, it took exception to the collective right of indigenous people to have 'their specific character reflected in the legal system and in the political institutions of their country', on the basis that 'the existence of indigenous populations in a country should not . . . give rise in every case to the creation of some kind of special political institutions'.[6]

One Canadian indigenous group suggested an expansion of this universal collective right to include indigenous participation in international institutions and to cover judicial as well as political domestic institutions so that 'where possible, the local system of justice should be controlled by the indigenous people themselves'.[7] They claimed their system of self-government in Canada was only a system of administrative enclaves circumscribed by national laws and budget programmes. But the Canadian Government, though affirming its policy of self-government for aboriginal communities, warned that States would be 'unlikely to support a principle that went beyond this and required that national political institutions and legal systems be redesigned to reflect the character of indigenous populations'.[8] Canada would prefer the declaration to deal with objectives founded on already recognised individual rights rather than newly formulated collective rights.

Professor Daes presented an even further expanded list of twenty-eight principles to the 1988 working group meeting. She hoped these principles could form a basis for a universal declaration of indigenous rights. At most, governments will agree to some notion of indigenous autonomy but not independence. There is little chance, however, that states with large indigenous populations will be party to any international convention that has binding effect. It is more likely that there will be a declaration that has no enforcement or supervision procedures. A declaration differs from a convention in international law in that it is not legally binding on ratifying states. It lends itself to more rhetorical statements including the recitation of goals and objectives.

Whereas Mr Coe and the Aboriginal groups generally found the twenty-eight principles too modest, the Australian Government, and presumably most other governments, found them too expansive. The draft declaration was rejected by the indigenous representatives because it was weak in its treatment of land, treaty and self-determination issues. The Australian Government would have no problem with the use of the terms 'peoples' and 'self-determination' in a declaration, provided it is accepted that indigenous peoples are part of the general population. The Australian Government argued that, as self-determination is a term adopted from the decolonisation process, it is not applicable to peoples within the democratic nation of Australia, which has been decolonised.[9]

The working group has now commissioned a study of treaties. At the seventh session in 1989, Aboriginal representatives called for international monitoring of the Australian treaty process, emphasising the need for a mutually accepted process. Little progress was made at this session as Daes thought she had received an insufficiently representative number of replies to warrant substantial revision of her text.

The Australian Government has published a detailed response to the Daes 1988 draft. It noted 'an element of drift in the WGIP's approach' and saw a need for meetings of indigenous organisations and governments 'to facilitate compromise and consensus'. The small print set down the strict parameters within which the Hawke Government has been prepared to allow the rhetoric of treaties and self-determination to have effect.

Draft principle 12 dealt with the right of ownership, possession and use of lands and resources that indigenous people have traditionally occupied or used. Australia had problems with the principle being extended to lands that had once been used by Aborigines but that were now owned by others because it could appear that the principle is referring to the whole continent. The principle declared that such lands could be taken away only with consent witnessed by a treaty or agreement. As if adopting Mr Howard's concerns back home, the Government submitted there was difficulty with the reference to 'treaties', 'since the term at international law means agreements concluded between states and governed by international law; this would exclude agreements concluded with indigenous peoples which form part of a nation'.[10]

Draft principle 14 dealt with indigenous ownership and control of resources located on people's traditional territory. Presumably including itself, the Australian Government said it was 'unlikely that Governments would surrender rights to control aspects of land use where possible changes may impact on others'. It is difficult to conceive a situation when there would be no impact on others.

Draft principle 15 dealt with claims procedures and compensation for land that cannot be restored to Aboriginal ownership. The Government said land claims were a State issue, there being 'no nationwide provision in Australia for the reclaiming of lands by Aboriginals'. Noting that compensation was an ill-defined concept they felt it 'unlikely that any Australian Government will accede to compensation for land resources which have been removed from possession'. Commenting on a later principle, the Australian Government said that 'compensation for past deprivation is unlikely to be acceptable to most governments; nor does it find foundation in existing international instruments'.

Some of the Aboriginal representatives have grown restless with the academic consideration of word formulations that expand every year. Shane Houston from NAIHO says he and other Aboriginal participants now see discussion about international standards as clouds simply floating above what is happening on the ground in Aboriginal communities. They want to know how debate in Geneva is going to help them in their efforts to keep their communities 'alive, together and Aboriginal'.[11] He rightly sees the risk that a declaration would be 'nothing more than a grand statement that does little more than make you feel nice and warm all over for a short time'.

There is a long road to travel before governments participating in the working group process will be party to a declaration acceptable to the Aboriginal representatives. There is no reason to believe that non-participating governments will be any more accommodating. Paul Coe has been Australia's strongest Aboriginal advocate for participation in the working group processes. In 1989 he conceded that 'international instruments have not legitimised the rights of indigenous peoples to talk in terms of collective rights'. But he continues to think that international fora are important 'because if we continue to work only in the domestic arena we will always be a captive and managed people'. The 1990 meeting achieved nothing other than more rarefied discussion about terms such as self-determination. It gave Robert Tickner the chance to place on record that successive Australian representatives had 'stressed the importance of the principle of self-determination for Aboriginal people in Australia'. He said ATSIC provided an unprecedented opportunity for Aborigines 'to determine and shape policy and to plan development based on the needs of local communities'. At the 1991 meeting, he hailed ATSIC as a significant step towards self-determination: 'For the first time in the administration of indigenous peoples' affairs, the power to allocate funding and to determine priorities at a national level has been taken largely out of the hands of governments and government officials and given over to the elected representatives of Aboriginal and Torres Strait Islander People.' He assured the group of the Australian Government's continued commitment to a Declaration of the Rights of Indigenous Peoples. The Working Group hopes to finalise its draft declaration in time for 1993, the International Year of World Indigenous Peoples. However, if it attracts broad support from the community of nations, it will bring little satisfaction to indigenous representatives wanting to assert independence and sovereignty distinct from the societies of their colonisers.

ILO Convention 107/169

Between 1986 and 1989, the International Labour Organisation (ILO) revised its 1957 convention dealing with indigenous and tribal peoples so as to make it less assimilationist. The Australian Government was involved at all stages, from the first meeting in 1986 to the consideration of the revision at the two general sessions that followed.

Bill Gray, now the Chief Executive Officer for ATSIC, attended as an Australian Government representative from the then Department of Aboriginal Affairs. All delegates agreed with him that indigenous peoples should have the right to retain their unique identity. The disagreement was over limits to power sharing, which would make the right effective. Some, like Gray, spoke of participation in existing State institutions, while others joined the call of the WCIP for indigenous control over social and economic developments. There was resistance to including the right of self-determination in the revised convention. Gray suggested that a distinction be made between internal and external self-determination, the former being a restricted right exercisable within the limits of the State. This held no appeal for the indigenous representatives who were unanimous in their insistence on the unqualified right. In the end the experts confined their recommendation to indigenous and tribal peoples having 'as much control as possible over their economic, social and cultural development'.

Three years later, still avoiding the unqualified term 'self-determination', the Australian Government, at the conclusion of the revision process, welcomed the shift from integration to respect for the identity of indigenous peoples. This policy change was consistent with the Government's own moves to provide Aborigines 'with greater autonomy and decision making powers within existing legislative and administrative structures'.[12] Although the Government was prepared to support the right to equal participation and to recognise indigenous laws and practices, it insisted that nothing in the revised convention should imply a collective right to self-determination as enshrined in the UN Charter and the international human rights conventions.

At the initial meeting in 1986 Aboriginal participants had submitted that the right of self-determination should be mentioned in the preamble of the convention. It was not. Instead, the preamble recognises the aspirations of indigenous and tribal peoples to control their institutions and to maintain their identities 'within the framework of the States in which they live'.

The original convention had spoken of 'populations'. In response to demands from indigenous groups, the ILO agreed to refer to 'peoples', adding a rider that the use of the term 'peoples' was not to be construed as having any implications in international law.[13] They wanted to avoid any promotion of separatist ideas.[14]

Three Aborigines, including Geoff Clarke (of the National Coalition of Aboriginal Organisations), attended the 1988 ILO conference but withdrew because there was insufficient consideration for the right of self-determination and the need for consent by indigenous peoples on matters affecting them. They felt more emphasis should have been placed on consultation, collaboration and participation with indigenous populations:

We define our rights in terms of self-determination. We are not looking to dismember your States and you know it. But we do insist on the right to control our territories, our resources, the organisation of our societies, our own decision-making instit-utions, and the maintenance of our own cultures and way of life. We are not asking for this right – it is our birthright.[15]

Clarke later said that the coalition was finding it difficult to be accorded its due status as 'the black provincial government of Australia'.[16] He attended the 1989 conference but came away bitterly disappointed at the Australian Government's conspiracy 'to undermine any principles the revision process may have established which would have recognised and protected indigenous peoples' rights'. The crunch came with the consideration of article 6, which provides that governments will consult with people 'whenever consideration is being given to legislative or administrative measures which may affect them directly'. Indigenous representatives insisted on the need for consent rather than consultation only.

Rejecting the revised convention on grounds that it does not set reasonable standards, Mr Clarke claimed that:

Academic and legalistic language used in the revision process and contained in the revised Convention has, in my opinion, been designed to restrict and retard the development of effective international principles relating to indigenous people which could be used as an effective international legal challenge to national policy.[17]

Future Directions

Aboriginal leaders who have trod the international circuit are yet to find any consolation from any convention or declaration. Satisfaction there will be a long time in coming, given that there are 300 million indigenous people in the world, many of whom do not enjoy even the processes of consultation espoused by the revised ILO convention 169. Those who reject domestic proposals in Australia on the basis that there are better pickings to be found in the international forum need to have a very long-term view.

Having failed to win concessions with the ILO convention, some Aboriginal leaders are pinning their hopes on a Declaration of Indigenous Rights. As a declaration, if it comes to be, it will not provide for any reporting or enforcement mechanisms. It will be simply a general statement of aspirational principles. It is this sort of statement at the domestic level that Mr Hawke has been espousing and that these leaders have condemned as hollow rhetoric. If unenforceable rhetoric is insufficient to meet Aboriginal demands at home, it must be equally irrelevant in the international forum, especially if it gains approval from many other governments only because they define indigenous peoples so as to exclude any groups resident in their territories.

One lawyer, Mr Tony Simpson, who has participated in most sessions of the working group through his association with NAILSS, has expressed the hope that the principles of the declaration could later be refined into a convention winning approval from the UN General Assembly. A convention recognising collective rights of indigenous people over and above the individual rights of minorities is not on any government's agenda. The chasm between a convention and a declaration was spelt out by the ILO observer at the seventh session of the working group in 1989. Justifying the restrictive terms of the ILO convention, he pointed out that it was intended to create binding agreements between States and as such had to be a set of minimal principles in order to attract wide ratification. A UN declaration, on the other hand, could go further in satisfying the aims of the relevant parties, not only by including the rights to which indigenous people were entitled, but also by including their goals and aspirations.[18]

Just as it is 200 years too late for a real treaty between Aborigines and settlers, it is 100 years too early for an international convention that would be acceptable to Aboriginal leaders and most governments. In the international forum, Aborigines will at best have a statement of their goals and aspirations that will be unenforceable and so general that it will always be arguable whether or not government policy complies. It will always remain simply a matter of argument.

There will be continuing debates about self-determination and sovereignty. It is important that participants avoid the trap of playing endless word games which do nothing to alleviate the plight of Aborigines alienated from the society that sets the terms of the games. In international law, self-determination has applied chiefly to people emerging from the colonisation process being guaranteed a choice of future. It is not allowed to just any group. There must be an inquiry 'whether there is enough homogeneity or unity or common desire to hold the state together; whether it has economic resources and political capacity'.[19] Though there is still no definition of 'peoples' in international law, the right of self-determination, carrying with it the entitlement to partition territory, is exercisable only by a discrete territorial community, the members of which are conscious of themselves as members of such a community. Full self-government is possible only for groups who are separate geographically.

Whatever the niceties of academic discussion, there is no way the international community of nations will agree to interference in their members' domestic affairs. It is unlikely that nation states will agree to outside agencies being able to adjudicate the claim of indigenous peoples to separate themselves from a nation state. This is even less likely when the nation and its boundaries have been recognised over a considerable length of time. Separation would be inconceivable in the case of an indigenous population scattered throughout the nation, made up of diverse groups without a long established nationwide political structure, and having intermarried with descendants of the settlers over centuries.

The sovereignty of Australia within its uncontested borders will never be questioned by the UN General Assembly or adjudicated by the International Court of Justice. The national self-interest of every member nation at the UN stands in the way of any such course being even theoretically possible. Australia, being recognised as a nation state occupying an entire continent, sharing no disputed boundaries, and having a self-identifying Aboriginal population that is increasingly urban-based, not living separate and apart from other Australians, and being less than 2 per cent of the population, is one of the countries least likely to have its internal dealings scrutinised by the assembly or the court. Any conceivable convention or legal procedure that would open Australia to such scrutiny without Government consent would draw most other states in its net too.

Aborigines have been strongly represented at the working group meetings. But there is no reason to believe they can win any more rounds in Geneva than they can win back home. There may be an emerging international consensus developing about the collective rights of indigenous peoples. But there is no evidence of it developing any more quickly in Geneva than it is in Canberra. Participation at Geneva is no substitute for negotiation in Canberra for the domestic equivalent of a declaration or even a convention with reporting and enforcement procedures. If a declaration of aspirations from Geneva has shame value in pressuring the Australian Government to make more concessions to Aborigines, more so should a bipartisan declaration of the Australian Parliament have moral force in holding future governments to the line. The chief value of the Geneva exercises may be the sustained contact and solidarity with other indigenous groups rather than the compromised texts that finally emerge.

For every Australian politician who feels pressured to support the Aboriginal cause by the expression of Aboriginal grievances in Geneva, there is another who hardens their resolve to put an end to all special measures. For the foreseeable future, the dynamic of international consultations between governments and indigenous organisations will be a stand-off in which Aboriginal representatives put their ambit claim for self-determination and sovereignty, and government ministers express support for indigenous autonomy and participation in the state while maintaining cultural identity.

If the term 'self-determination' remains in Ms Daes' draft, it will still have many hurdles to face, by which time it will be so qualified as to present no obstacle and even no shame to the nation states that finally espouse the virtues of the declaration. Even the use of the term 'peoples' rather than 'populations' is likely to be qualified in the same way as it is in the new ILO convention, following a request from the New Zealand Government at the 1989 working group meeting.

The Australian Government's participation in the working group processes and its encouragement of Aboriginal involvement are indicators of its assessment that it has little to fear in the draft running its course, whether or not the term self-determination is included. Recent events in Eastern Europe will have done little to increase Soviet enthusiasm for the international recognition of collective indigenous rights. But even the USSR welcomed Australia's election to the UN Commission on Human Rights in May 1990, praising Australia's record on human rights. The Australian Government's participation in the first seven sessions of the Working Group on Indigenous Populations (as it is still formally known, despite indigenous peoples' objections) was sufficiently creditable not to disentitle Australia from election to this human rights commission, which has overall accountability for the working group. At the eighth session in 1990, Australia was the only government to make a substantive contribution to the drafting process.

Any international declaration dealing with the collective rights of indigenous or ethnic groups to self-determination is sure to be sufficiently circumscribed as to preclude internationally arbitrated claims by discrete territorial groups asserting independence, such as those in Bougainville, East Timor, and the various Soviet satellites, let alone groups who define themselves as the first nations living in fourth-world conditions.

FIVE:

OVERSEAS ATTEMPTS TO AGREE

Given that Geneva declarations will not achieve or even express any more than what national governments are already prepared to do or concede to indigenous people within their borders, there is a need to find new ways in Australia to talk about and to act on Aboriginal claims. Often people of goodwill despair as they survey the community of nations and lament that no nation has got it right; no indigenous people is satisfied with the treatment and recognition given by government. To try anything new or to think new thoughts is seen as an exercise in opening new conflicts and exposing old wounds rather than providing the hope of reconciliation. Although raising false hopes and expectations does nothing for Aborigines and heightens the animosity of their critics, it may be possible to learn from the experience of two nations with some similarities to our own.

A survey of recent initiatives on the part of New Zealand and Canada could provide us with some pointers and show up some now avoidable traps. Although both have made their mistakes, they have also made some creative moves in recent years. Like Australia, New Zealand and Canada were British colonies. However their relations with the indigenous inhabitants of their countries have been very different from our own, ensuring that indigenous claims have been more central to their ongoing national political agenda. The colonial authorities there negotiated treaties at the time of colonisation, which have formed the basis for negotiation between indigenous leaders and the national governments in recent years. Although these treaties have not provided any lasting solution to indigenous claims they have been instrumental in educating the general population about the legitimacy of those claims. They have even helped put indigenous rights on the national agenda for law reform. Canada and New Zealand have been experimenting with new ways to recognise the collective entitlements of the indigenous peoples within their national boundaries to determine their own future.

New Zealand

The Treaty of Waitangi was signed on 6 February 1840. There were two versions, one in English, the other in Maori. The Maori version reaffirmed Maori *tino rangatiratanga*. This term has no accurate English translation nor established jurisprudential content, but implies independence and perhaps even sovereignty. Protection was given to Maori land, villages, and all valued aspects of the Maori way of life. In return the British Crown was granted the power of *kawanatanga*, which some argue was only 'a subordinate power aimed primarily at achieving law and order among Pakeha (European) settlers'.[1] But according to the English version of the treaty, Maori ceded their sovereignty to the Crown in return for continued, undisturbed use of their lands, fisheries and forests for as long as they wished.

The treaty was not viewed as part of the domestic law of New Zealand. During the treaty's centenary year in 1940, the Privy Council heard argument in a case and even heard argument from a Maori who was not a lawyer, who urged the law lords besieged by war not to allow English law to be used to exert might over right. The English law lords were in no doubt: treaty rights could not be enforced in the courts unless they had been incorporated in the municipal law.[12] And so it was for the next thirty-five years.

In response to increased political activity by Maori and

increasing community awareness of the place of Maori culture in New Zealand life and identity, the Parliament enacted the Treaty of Waitangi Act in 1975. This Act bound the Crown. It set up a three-member tribunal chaired by the Chief Judge of the Maori Land Court. Maori individuals or groups could bring a complaint to the tribunal if they were likely to be prejudicially affected by any Act of Parliament, government policy, practice, act or omission occurring after the commencement of the Act. The tribunal had no power to make enforceable decisions but it could recommend action to government for compensation or removal of the prejudice. Also the Parliament could refer any proposed legislation to the tribunal for its consideration and recommendations and a minister could refer any proposed regulations to be made by the executive.

By 1984 Maori of all political persuasions were united in calling for a strengthening of the treaty and a groundswell of community support allowed the Labour Party to campaign on this platform. Elected in August 1984, the Lange Government took steps for further recognition of the treaty. The Treaty of Waitangi Amendment Act 1985 increased the tribunal to seven members, of whom four had to be Maori and the old tribunal ceased to exist. The new tribunal members did not sit until November 1986. Thereafter Maori could bring complaints claiming prejudicial treatment from government for anything done or not done since 1840.

The Lange Government was also committed to the new economic policies championed by their Minister for Finance, Roger Douglas. A central plank of 'Rogernomics' was the divesting of Crown assets to corporations for use and development. The State Owned Enterprises Act 1986 set up the machinery for the transfer of 10 million hectares of State-owned land to State enterprises established by the Act. Once transferred, these lands would not be available for return to Maori through claims procedures in the Maori Land Court. However the Act required the Crown to act in a manner consistent with the principles of the Treaty of

Waitangi. Once the government started the transfer process, litigation was commenced by the New Zealand Maori Council.

Sir Robin Cooke, the President of the High Court, saw the case as 'perhaps as important for the future of our country as any that has come before a New Zealand court'. The court reached a unanimous decision that was a victory for the Maori. The effect of the judgment was that the State Owned Enterprises Act had to be administered in such a way that Maori land claims were safeguarded. The court left it to the 'treaty partners, represented in this Court by the Government and the Maori Council', to work out the details. The parties later reported a settlement that gladdened the court. The agreement was that if land were transferred to a state enterprise, the Waitangi Tribunal could still recommend its return to Maori. Having said that the treaty signified a partnership between races, President Cooke expressed the court's hope 'that this momentous agreement will be a good augury for the future of the partnership'.[3] The court found itself in uncharted waters. It took account of political developments having noted that in earlier years there had been an emphasis on integration and the amalgamation of races, whereas now the emphasis was much more on Maoritanga (Maori identity), Maori land and communal life and a distinctive Maori identity.

Anxious to avoid paralysis of government economic activity in the wake of numerous Maori claims, President Cooke said that the principles of the treaty required the partners to act towards each other reasonably and with the utmost good faith.[4] Transfers of land could be made once the Crown acting reasonably and in good faith was satisfied that known or foreseeable Maori claims would not require retention of the land in question. The vague test of reasonableness vests judges with extraordinary discretion because the yardstick of reasonableness is not the actual words of the treaty (given its differing translations) but its principles, which are not to be found in either text.

Some Maori and their supporters claim that this judicial discretion has been applied to retard the real political and economic gains that Maori expected from the new treaty arrangements. But Sir Robin Cooke says this is to under-estimate the progress that Maori have made in litigation on the treaty. Maori critics claim the Waitangi Tribunal is now overloaded, under-resourced, bureaucratic, legalistic, and increasingly Pakeha dominated.

The second big case on the renewed treaty involved a Maori claim to fisheries. The Maori litigants obtained a $10m payout and a guaranteed 10 per cent share of the fisheries quota for the next four years. This case indicates that tribunal and court decisions could bring about a substantial redistribution of economic and political bargaining power in favour of the Maori. This is a novel role for judges, one with which Sir Robin Cooke has expressed some disquiet. He says the courts have an extremely delicate task in trying to balance and achieve some middle way between the conflicting arguments.

The Waitangi Tribunal was in its heyday from 1983 to 1986 when it denied the relinquishment of Maori sovereignty. Following recent court decisions, it has had to accept that Maori sovereignty ended in 1840. Pakeha settlement rights cannot now be denied in the tribunal.[5] The tribunal was able to indulge in inflated rhetoric before the 1985 amendment Act. Such rhetoric now would render it a dead letter with governments and their electors who have put the brakes on treaty developments. By the 1990 election it was clear that Labour's treaty policy was an electoral liability. Prior to that election, in May 1989, the Labour Government produced five principles for Crown action on the Treaty of Waitangi:

1 Kawanatanga: the Crown right to govern and make laws, or sovereignty, subject to Maori interests being accorded an appropriate priority.
2 Rangatiratanga iwi: more self-management and control over

those resources they wish to retain.

3 Equality: British law was selected by the treaty and makes Pakeha and Maori equal citizens.

4 Co-operation: consultation should occur on major issues of common concern and requires mutual good faith, balance and common sense.

5 Redress: the Crown, having provided a process for resolution of grievances, expects reconciliation to result.

Self-management, consultation, and equality under British law are the most that the major political parties in New Zealand are now prepared to grant Maori by way of self-determination, however much academic debate there be about *tino rangatiratanga*. Even the Labour Government, which pioneered the expansion of the tribunal's role, came to accept that tribunal recommendations would be reviewed in the light of economic constraints and community acceptance of the treaty at the ballot box. These constraints have not been absent from judicial minds either. In one 1989 decision, President Cooke said:

Maori must recognise that...both the history and the economy of the nation rule out extravagant claims in the democracy now shared. Both partners should know that a narrow focus on the past is useless. The principles of the Treaty have to be applied to give fair results in today's world.[6]

The tribunal is now sitting in up to four divisions at a time. It has sixteen members of whom eight are Maori Land Court judges. There are only four Maori judges in the country but there are now 150 Maori lawyers many of whom are experienced in putting cases to the tribunal. The South Island claim ran for over two years; the transcript stands twenty-seven feet high, and it includes 200 discrete grievances. No matter what recommendations are made by the tribunal nor what guidelines of reasonableness the courts enunciate, the bottom line will be what the Pakeha are prepared to concede, whatever their motives. When visiting New Zealand in 1990, Tiga Bayles from the New South Wales Land Council, wondered whether his people might in fact be better off for not having signed a treaty. He could 'not see any real benefits on this side of the water for having signed a treaty'.

Despite Bayles' despairing view, there is now a range of New Zealand legislation that requires administrators to take into account the principles of the treaty. For example, the Town and Country Planning Act requires planning authorities to consider the relationship of the Maori people and their culture and traditions with their ancestral lands. There is potential for Maori aspirations to be taken into account in Government decisions across the board. But in the end, as former Labour Prime Minister Palmer said: 'It must be clear that the government will make final decisions on treaty issues.' For many Maori this is intolerable. But for others it offers the prospect of their full participation in what Chief Justice Cooke has described as 'the democracy built upon the partnership for which the treaty stands'.

Even amongst Maori there are prominent citizens who see the treaty as undermining the very partnership it is supposed to effect. Mr Winston Peters, a Maori and a member of the conservative National Party, sees the treaty as 'a security blanket for many Maori, a talisman for failure'. Labelled an Uncle Tom by Maori activists, he has campaigned for the removal of the treaty, which he believes perpetuates Pakeha guilt and Maori anger:[7]

Why do my people also make up the disproportionate share of the educational failures, the unemployed, the welfare beneficiaries, the prison inmates, the youth suicides, the sick and infirm?

It is not enough to blame the alleged violation of the Treaty of Waitangi for these ills. These ills that afflict our young people especially are as much a Maori problem as they are a matter of

Government policy. The treaty cannot and will not dominate the future development of this nation.

We are all – every race, every creed, every colour – we are all equal partners in the future of New Zealand.[8]

In time the Parliament, the courts and the administration may not be seen as foreign Pakeha institutions but as the structures within which a meaningful partnership is lived out. These institutions will need to function in a manner which is seen to be reasonable and in utmost good faith not only by Pakeha politicians and judges but also by Maori who still find themselves marginalised from the dominant settler culture.

There is no way that any Australian government seeking bipartisan support and general community acceptance will contemplate a tribunal with the breadth of powers of the Waitangi Tribunal. Neither would they vest Australian courts with such wide discretion to determine a fair and reasonable distribution of resources between Aborigines and other Australians. The New Zealand experience highlights the considerable limits on what is achievable. Given Australia's history and the more diverse groupings of Aborigines and Islanders, Australia will not even come close to what New Zealand has put in place.

Canada

It was commonplace for the British Crown to enter into peace and friendship treaties with the Indians on the east coast of North America during the early eighteenth century. These treaties did not involve an extinguishment of native land title nor did they interfere with native social systems. Given the English – French conflicts and wars, it was in the interests of the European powers to bring about friendly relations with the Indians if only to ensure their neutrality.

After the defeat of the French, King George III enacted

the Royal Proclamation of 1763, which claimed sovereign dominion over all lands occupied by the French and which reserved to the 'several Nations or Tribes of Indians' their hunting grounds to the west of the rivers which drained into the Atlantic:

And whereas great Frauds and Abuses have been committed in purchasing Lands of the Indians, to the great Prejudice of our Interests, and to the great Dissatisfaction of the said Indians; In order, therefore, to prevent such Irregularities for the future, and to the end that the Indians may be convinced of our Justice and determined Resolution to remove all reasonable Cause of Discontent, We do, with the Advice of our Privy Council strictly enjoin and require, that no private Person do presume to make any purchase from the said Indians of any Lands reserved to the said Indians, within those parts of our Colonies where, We have thought proper to allow Settlement; but that, if at any Time any of the Said Indians should be inclined to dispose of the said Lands, the same shall be Purchased only for Us, in our Name, at some public Meeting or Assembly of the said Indians, to be held for that Purpose by the Governor or Commander in Chief of our Colony respectively within which they shall lie; and in case they shall lie within the limits of any Proprietary Government, they shall be purchased only for the Use and in the name of such Proprietaries, conformable to such Directions and Instructions as We or they shall think proper to give for that Purpose.[9]

Following the procedures set down in the proclamation, land cession treaties were negotiated as the colonial frontier extended west and north across modern-day Canada. The British North America Act 1867, which provided for confederation, gave the Federal Government exclusive responsibility for 'Indians and lands reserved for the Indians'. It also provided for the acquisition of Rupert's Land (which covered all of modern Manitoba, most of Saskatchewan, northern Quebec and Ontario, southern Alberta and part of the Northwest Territories) from the

Hudson Bay Company. The Canadian Government had to assume responsibility for the protection and well being of the region's aboriginal residents. Thereafter the Federal Government passed the Indian Act in 1876, which has been periodically redrafted and which provides for the administration of Indian reserves and the rights of status Indians. The present Indian Act was passed in 1951. Between 1871 and 1923 the Government concluded Indian treaties that covered most of the Indian lands in Ontario and the three prairie provinces. Indian title to land was purchased and extinguished in return for lump sum payments, annuities, services, hunting and fishing rights and security of Indian reserves. The reserve areas were fixed by a formula that permitted one square mile per family of five. Whenever land was required for development or pastoral expansion, a treaty would be negotiated. Indians on the other lands were left undisturbed. Assimilation and equality were the aims of legislative reforms to the Indian Acts culminating in the 1969 White Paper, which was rejected by aboriginal leaders. An Indian Claims Commission was then set up to deal with grievances.

In 1973 the Supreme Court of Canada gave its decision in the landmark case *Calder* v *Attorney-General of British Columbia*.[10] Though the bench split evenly on the question of whether or not the royal proclamation of 1763 applied to lands in British Columbia (to the west of the Rockies), the court was unequivocal in its recognition of aboriginal land title. Being of the view that the proclamation did not apply to British Columbia, Justice Judson outlined the legal result of the history of European settlement. He accepted without question that when the settlers came, the Indians were there, organised in societies and occupying the land as their ancestors had done for centuries. So Indians had the right to continue to live on their lands as their ancestors had lived. That would remain the case until the right was lawfully extinguished by the sovereign. This right remained 'dependent on the goodwill of the sovereign'.[11]

There was no question about the pre-existence of the right nor about its recognition. The only issue was whether or not the Indian title had ever been effectively extinguished by the Crown. In the other major judgment of the court, Justice Hall said 'the proposition that after conquest or discovery the native peoples have no rights except those subsequently granted or recognised by the conqueror or discoverer' was 'wholly wrong'.[12] The bench also divided over whether Indian title could be extinguished by the general land enactments of the Province Parliament or only by enactments that specifically mentioned Indian title.

The existence in Canadian law and the recognition by their courts of Indian native title has given weight to the political claims of Indians that they deserve recognition as the owners of unceded lands and that they deserve compensation for any title that is now to be extinguished by unilateral action of the Crown. The issue comes to life each time there is a large commercial project planned for unceded lands in remote areas inhabited mainly by Indians. Since 1975, five land claims agreements have been negotiated between the Crown and Indian interests.[13] The main focus is now on the two territories that are sparsely populated, especially above 60 degrees north latitude, and that are likely to be rich in minerals. For example, after eight years of negotiations, an agreement in principle was signed by the Prime Minister, the President of the Dene Nation and the President of the North West Territories Metis Association, recognising Indian title to 180 000 square kilometres and providing cash compensation of $500m for extinguishment of aboriginal title throughout the other vast traditional lands of the people, and a share in resource royalties. These agreements are part of the Canadian Government's 'Northern Political and Economic Framework', which is aimed at promoting northern economic development by utilisation of vast oil and gas resources and affirming Canadian sovereignty. Federal programmes are being handed over to territorial governments at the same time. The framework is 'a response to northerners' aspirations for responsibility over their own affairs and to the nation's need for a strong and viable Canadian community north of 60°'. Its objective is 'to provide a stable and fair regime for industry resulting in the encouragement of the timely development of the north's substantial resources'.[14]

The Supreme Court of Canada gave even greater weight to Indian claims in its 1985 decision *Guerin* v *The Queen*.[15] Justice Dickson said that both substantive judgments (of Justices Judson and Hall) delivered in Calder were authority for the proposition 'that aboriginal title existed in Canada (at least where it has not been extinguished by appropriate legislative action) independently of the Royal Proclamation of 1763'.[16] Justice Judson had proceeded on the basis that the Royal Proclamation was not the exclusive source of Indian title, and Justice Hall on the basis that 'aboriginal Indian title does not depend on treaty, executive order or legislative enactment'.

In the Guerin case the question was whether or not the Crown owed a duty to the Indian band to protect their interests once Government officials had negotiated a lease of the band's reserve land to a golf club. The Crown argued that its duty was a public law duty that could not be enforced by individuals in the courts. By various means of argument, all judges held that the Crown's duty to the Indian band was enforceable by them.

Speaking for four members of the bench, Justice Dickson said that British courts had established that change in the sovereign does not in general affect the title of aboriginal peoples to their land. Upon the assertion of British sovereignty, existing interests in land were recognised by the Crown until they were dealt with by Parliament or the executive. Indian land rights were not personal rights because they could not be transferred to a third party; they could only be surrendered to the Crown. Upon the assertion of British sovereignty, Indians retained a legal right to occupy and possess their lands, though the ultimate title was now vested in the Crown.[17] Dickson decided that the Indians' interest in land gives rise to an obligation of trust on the Crown that exists independent of any action by the legislative or executive branches of government.[18]

It was the Crown's ongoing obligation that explained the 'inalienability' of the Indian interest in land. Indians could not sell off their land interests to others; they could only surrender their title to the Crown. This was to facilitate the Crown's ability to represent the Indians in dealings with third parties.

In the other major judgment of the court, Justice Wilson found that it was not legislation of the Canadian Parliament that created the Crown's obligation; rather legislation 'recognises the existence of such an obligation ... [which] has its roots in the aboriginal title of Canada's Indians'.[19] Though she saw the Indian interest in land as a limited one, it was one nonetheless that the Crown had to consider in the utilisation of the lands.

This developing jurisprudence from Canada's highest court has established that Indian land claims are not matters of welfare or compensation for past injustice but recognition of existing entitlements under the law and compensation for land rights that are being extinguished by agreement between the Crown and Indian representatives. The Crown as sovereign has the right to extinguish property rights. But under the rule of law, such rights should be extinguished only by consent or by compulsory acquisition if the common good dictates, and then only on payment of just compensation. Until land rights are extinguished, the Crown has an obligation to the Indians for the lands it holds for them.[20]

In November 1981 every provincial government in Canada except for Quebec joined in an accord with the Federal Government for the patriation of a revised constitution that would no longer be an Act of the British Parliament. The Meech Lake accord was an attempt to reach an agreement with Quebec to submit to the new confederation. The attempt under the agreement failed but Quebec would have been guaranteed constitutional recognition as a 'distinct society' able to promote and protect French language and culture. As part of the process, the Prime Minister and all ten Premiers agreed to negotiate a 'Canada clause' for the constitution addressing the rights of aborigines, the multicultural nature of Canada and the relationship between its English and French speaking cultures.

The Constitution Act 1982 includes the new Canadian Charter of Rights and Freedoms, which codifies fundamental freedoms, democratic rights, mobility rights, legal rights, equality rights and minority language educational rights. The charter is the first part of the seven-part Act. The briefest part is part II concerning the rights of the indigenous peoples of Canada. Section 35 originally provided that existing aboriginal and treaty rights be recognised and affirmed, and that for the purposes of the Act 'aboriginal peoples of Canada' includes the Indian, Inuit and Metis peoples of Canada.

In 1980 the Federal Government had courted indigenous support by making a commitment to constitutional recognition of aboriginal rights. The provincial governments originally wanted to omit any reference to these rights, but the Supreme Court said that the provinces had to be involved in any such process. Conservative Premier Lougheed from Alberta put up a compromise qualifying the rights to be recognised and affirmed, adding the word 'existing', thereby ensuring that the constitutional provision did not create any rights nor form the basis for their development. The provision was simply to ensure that the constitution did not derogate any rights that happened to exist. Putting aboriginal rights on hold, the Premiers agreed to a series of First Ministers' Conferences to consider 'constitutional matters that directly affect the aboriginal peoples of Canada', including the identification and definition of their rights to be included in the constitution.

There were four such conferences held between 1983 and 1987, with minimal progress.

Seventeen parties participated in these conferences. They included the Federal Government, the governments of the ten provinces and the two territories and four national aboriginal organisations. Like our Northern Territory, the two Canadian territories are remote, sparsely populated and subject to extreme climatic conditions. The Yukon Territory bordering on Alaska has a population of only 25 000 people, one-quarter of whom are Indians. The North West Territories covers a vast 3.4 million square kilometres with a population of only 53 000 of whom only 42 per cent are European, largely confined to the Mackenzie Valley. In the arctic regions, the Inuit (Eskimos) are in the majority.

The four national organisations represent the vast variety of aboriginal interests in Canada. The Assembly of First Nations represents the 580 Indian bands made up of the 330 000 status Indians subject to the Indian Act. Seventy per cent of these Indians still live on the 2252 reserves. During preparations for the first First Ministers' Conference in 1983, there was division among chiefs about tactics and participation. This resulted in the withdrawal of some chiefs and the setting up of the Coalition of First Nations. By 1985 there were further disagreements resulting in another breakaway group, the Prairie Treaty Nations Alliance. The prairie provinces of Alberta, Saskatchewan and Manitoba were covered by Indian treaties between 1871 and 1908. These treaties still provide rights and entitlements for treaty Indians and are the basis for specific claims and ongoing negotiations for land settlements. Treaty Indians have filed 532 specific claims since 1972, of which 43 have been decided or settled and 21 have been suspended. The registered Indians from the terrritories and British Columbia are outside treaty areas. They make comprehensive claims for land settlements, of which only five have been settled. Their claims take from one to ten years. The processes and possible outcomes for comprehensive and specific claims

are very different as comprehensive claims entail negotiations afresh, with no reference to pre-existing treaties,
and nowadays there is no insistence that all pre-existing
title be extinguished. Mr Jean Chretien QC, who was
Minister of Indian Affairs and Northern Development when
the comprehensive land claims process was set up, has
described the policy:

Recognising that the claims were not simply exchanges of the
Aboriginal interest for land and money, the policy stipulated that
the settlement must contribute positively to a lasting solution of
cultural, social and economic problems that for too long have kept
the Indian and Inuit peoples in a disadvantaged position within
the larger Canadian society. [21]

Given the different political agenda of the Indian groups
covered by treaties and land claim settlements, it was no
surprise to see separate representative organisations
emerge. But the Government continued to deal with the
assembly as the representative body for the Indians.

The Native Council of Canada (NCC) used to represent
Metis and non-status Indians that, it claimed, numbered
more than 1 million. Before 1985, an Indian woman lost that
status if she married a non-Indian and her children could
not be status Indians. Those who renounced their status and
left reserves in earlier years could acquire the rights of
citizenship and become non-status Indians. Before 1960
Indians could vote in Canadian elections only if they
renounced their status. In 1985 the Federal Government
legislated to permit women in mixed marriages to regain
their Indian status, which could also be enjoyed by the
children of the marriage. The NCC draws its support from
Indians in the more urban areas. When both their seats for
the 1983 First Ministers' Conference were allocated to non-
status Indians, the Metis National Council was set up to
represent the 398 000 Metis who are people of mixed Indian
and French descent mainly from the west. Most Metis do

not have a recognised land base. The 28 000 Inuit who live in fifty permanent settlements located north of the tree line in northern Quebec, Labrador and the Northern Territories were represented by the Inuit Committee on National Issues.

The aboriginal organisations saw self-government as the issue for First Ministers' Conferences from the beginning. Section 91(24) of the British North America Act 1867 (since renamed the Constitution Act 1867) provided the Dominion Parliament with exclusive legislative authority over 'Indians, and Lands reserved for the Indians'. The only breakthroughs made by the aboriginal organisations were the guarantee of consultation at a First Ministers' Conference prior to any amendment of section 91(24) or the rights in the 1982 constitution, the inclusion of rights under land claims agreements in the constitutional protection provision, and equality of treatment for Indian women and men. There was also provision made for future First Ministers' Conferences.

By the time of the second First Ministers' Conference in 1984, the Canadian House of Commons had received an all party committee report recommending constitutional recognition of the aboriginal right to self-government. The report saw this right as inherent in the Indian first nations. Prime Minister Trudeau put up a formula for the recognition of the right to self-governing institutions. The powers were to be negotiated between the relevant aboriginal groups, provincial and federal governments. Only three provinces supported the proposal, well short of the two-thirds necessary for constitutional amendment. Aboriginal leaders were not enthusiastic anyway, as Trudeau had admitted the amendment would have little meaning in law. At the third conference in 1985, the new Prime Minister Brian Mulroney proposed that Indian self-government could be granted under federal and provincial agreements. Saskatchewan wanted negotiation to be optional for the provinces. This attracted the support of two-thirds of the provinces but the

Assembly of First Nations would not agree. Mulroney was unable to win aboriginal support.

The last conference was held in 1987. The aboriginal organisations were insistent on the recognition of their inherent right to self-government without the need to negotiate with the provincial and federal governments. For their part, the more sympathetic governments were prepared to support a right of self-government, contingent on satisfactory negotiation of powers. Mulroney presented a draft proposal to provide the 'aboriginal peoples of Canada' with 'the right to self-government within the context of the Canadian federation'.[22] Under this proposal, provincial governments would have been obliged to negotiate terms and conditions of aboriginal self-government.

All four aboriginal organisations rejected the proposal because it did not recognise the inherent right to self-government that they claimed to have existed untrammelled before and since any imperial or Canadian legislation. Mr George Erasmus, head of the Assembly of First Nations, argued that self-government was already included in 'the existing aboriginal and treaty rights' recognised and affirmed by section 35 of the 1982 Constitution Act'. The recognition or creation of a right, contingent on provincial government agreement would add nothing and might even derogate from existing rights. The aboriginal organisations issued a joint proposal for indigenous self-government. An opinion poll at this time indicated that 77 per cent of Canadians favoured the right of aboriginal Canadians to govern themselves.

In June 1987, within a month of the breakdown of discussions about aboriginal self-government, the federal and provincial governments stitched up the Meech Lake accord. It allowed three years for all provinces to agree to Quebec's being recognised as a 'distinct society'. Aboriginal organisations saw this as a double standard. They argued that if any groups had a claim to be recognised as distinct societies, Indians and Inuit, (who even under the British enjoyed recognition and protection of their separateness) ought to be included. In early 1990, with time running out on the three-year deadline for the doomed accord, various proposals were put forward by the provincial governments. The provinces of Manitoba and Newfoundland and Labrador both suggested the inclusion of a 'Canada clause' in the constitution that would recognise aboriginal people and the multicultural dimension of the Canadian heritage. A Special Committee of the Canadian House of Commons reported in May 1990 and encouraged 'the First Ministers to respond to these fundamental elements of Canada by recognising them in the body of the Constitution'.[23]

Though there has been much political debate about the need to enshrine the right of aboriginal self-government in the Canadian constitution, there has been no agreement even amongst aboriginal groups about the content of the right. The only thing that is clear 'is that no single approach or model will meet the needs or aspirations of all aboriginal peoples. A "universal formula" is doomed to failure'.[24] Constitutional recognition will be the outcome of continued political agitation motivated by the negotiation of land claims settlements in areas of national commercial value, and underpinned by the Supreme Court's reconfirmation of the enduring reality of aboriginal rights to land and resources, subject to the dominion of the State.

In 1990 in *Sparrow* v *The Queen*, the Canadian Supreme Court considered the aboriginal rights clause of the Charter of Freedoms and its application to fisheries legislation, which purported to limit the size of nets to be used by all fishermen, including Indians. Mr Sparrow, an Indian, challenged the legislation. The court found that 'Section 35(1), at the least, provides a solid constitutional base upon which subsequent negotiations can take place. It also affords aboriginal peoples constitutional protection against provincial legislative power'. The court adopted the view that the provision 'calls for a just settlement for aboriginal peoples. It renounces the old rules of the game under which the Crown established courts of law and denied those courts the authority to question sovereign claims made by the Crown'. The judges described the vague provision as 'a solemn commitment that must be given meaningful content'.

In Australia, major conflicts with Aboriginal landholders and traditional owners will not be resolvable until we Australians have also made a solemn commitment that can be given meaningful content. At the national level it is inevitable that there will be a variety of aboriginal groups wanting to represent their diverse constituencies and to negotiate on their terms. There is no prospect of a government-sponsored and funded body being the sole representative or even chief negotiator on behalf of different indigenous groups. It would be folly to expect ATSIC to command assent from all Aboriginal groups. No matter what its resources, it will not be seen as the only Aboriginal mouthpiece. The Canadian experience is that in a federation, the national government cannot find a resolution to these issues unless the state and territory governments are involved. The national government must give special regard to the needs and interests of the remote territories that do not yet enjoy full self-government and that have a higher percentage of indigenous inhabitants. Given a constitutional provision, which acknowledges existing indigenous rights, courts can play a creative role in investigating the limits of those rights and striking the balance on a case by case basis, effecting more justice for individuals than can parliaments passing laws and bureaucrats designing regulations to cover all situations. Canadians have appreciated that there is a need to strike a balance, preserving some traditional rights as they have been understood and practised by indigenous people for a long time. Australian politicians continue to take the broad brush approach, presuming that such traditional rights are long gone or creations of fertile romantic imaginations.

Conclusion:

THE WAY FORWARD TO 2001

All Australians have inherited a tragic history with regards to Aborigines – a sad and sorry history that still has ongoing effects of dispersal, dispossession, and loss of culture and kinship. The nation built on this dispossession has an obligation and a self-interest in setting right what it can and providing support for Aboriginal communities as the custodians of their culture and heritage. In many country towns, white as well as black Australians feel powerless to stop the prejudice in their children's playgrounds. They can make no claim to live together in harmony and peace. In tough economic times, it is particularly difficult to express any civic pride or to break down the barriers. Meanwhile, the poor whites and the blacks in these towns have so much in common, especially their powerlessness, their lack of options and increasingly their identity with the local area. As the local oral Aboriginal histories of so-called settlement get set down in writing and as even the better-off whites come to know the story of the 'Blackfellow Creek' or the 'Massacre Creek' on the outskirts of their own town, people are beginning to understand their local history from both sides of the river. They want to be able to draw the line on the past and make a fresh start in race relations. They want to be able to live together, owning their history and shaping a better future for their children in the playground. This local concern is a national preoccupation. National strategies must be able to complement local initiatives, although they are not a substitute.

Neither land rights nor any constitutional amendment is going to provide a quick-fix solution to the problems confronting Aborigines in contemporary Australia. However the shape of Australian society and the place of Aborigines can be determined, in part, by the legal structures that protect and enhance Aboriginal values, perspectives and relationships with the environment and other Australians. Symbolism is important, though it is no substitute for material resources and changed mindsets. In time, however, national symbols can effect a change in those who administer power in the various branches of government, and between those other Australians who relate constantly with Aborigines, especially in country towns. In time, too, these changes will be reflected in government funding priorities and in community acceptance of programmes targeted at alleviating the plight of Aborigines. There is no symbolic moment on the national calender now until 1 January 2001. Now is the time to lay the groundwork for change. Before any symbolic action, including any instrument of reconciliation, can be finalised, all outstanding land rights issues need to be resolved guaranteeing communities permanent control and enjoyment of their ancestral lands. If that were done, there might be sufficient good faith shown to Aborigines to demonstrate that reconciliation is not a cheap substitute for justice. Rather, justice is a precondition for reconciliation.

When investigating the legal feasibility of a makarrata back in 1982, the Senate Committee travelled Australia hearing submissions from interested citizens. At Alice Springs, there was a strong interchange between Senator Gareth Evans and Phillip Toyne, then solicitor for the Pitjantjatjara people. Toyne, doubting the benefits to be gained from either side in Canberra when it came to treaty talk, posed the rhetorical question:

If the Liberal Government as it now stands has not been prepared to back Aboriginal interests over a whole series of issues with various State governments, then what chance has a Makarrata got of achieving anything meaningful in the way of compensation?[1]

Gareth Evans saw the process rather than the outcome as important. Confirmed in his fears, Toyne asked: 'What does that really mean in terms of the rights of Aboriginal people to achieve and control land?'[2] The same questions could be asked today of the Hawke Government in its fourth term. National land rights is not on the agenda. Neither is an agreement that contains provision for compensation for lost land. However, some advocates are prepared to play another word-game and equate special government programmes for Aborigines with compensation for lost land. Such programmes in education, training, health and employment are equally available to Aboriginal communities who have not lost their land and to those who now enjoy legal recognition of their title to land. The provision of basic services and affirmative action programmes should not be equated with compensation.

There is still a need for law reform in Tasmania and Western Australia to provide suitable title for Aboriginal landholdings generally. In all other States except New South Wales, there is still a need for land rights legislation allowing the dispossessed to claim land on the basis of traditional or historical association. There is still no claims process over unalienated crown land outside the Northern Territory, New South Wales and Queensland. There may still be a need for a National Land Claims Tribunal to adjudicate land claims by Aborigines who gain no satisfaction from State legislation. Unfortunately the Hawke Government has now withdrawn even its promises to provide land in States where local land rights legislation is inadequate. In his 1991 address to the Working Group on Indigenous Populations, Robert Tickner said the Commonwealth 'remains committed to addressing the remaining unmet land needs of Aboriginal people in the Northern Territory'. No such pledge was made for dispossessed

Aborigines in the States. Although he was critical of Queensland and Tasmania, Tickner could only express the hope that the States would reconsider their legislation. He did not even make a veiled threat of Commonwealth action.

There is no reason why the Commonwealth could not legislate to provide security of existing Aboriginal land-holdings in State jurisdictions. A Commonwealth law could provide that Aboriginal land in the States was not to be resumed by either the State or the Commonwealth government unless there were first a report made to the Commonwealth Parliament outlining the case for resumption by compulsory acquisition for unavoidable public purposes. There could be a legislative device to vest the land automatically in an Aboriginal land trust should either House of Parliament not agree to the resumption within a fixed period of time. Such a law, though complex, could be enacted so as to honour the suggestion put by the Australian Government representative to the ILO committee of experts in 1986 to restrict state power to acquire land 'except where clearly necessary and there are no alternatives, as established by some public inquiry which guarantees the right of the indigenous population to participate in that inquiry'.[3] In any event, the Commonwealth Parliament needs to legislate to preclude the possibility of resumption of Aboriginal land by executive action of the Commonwealth Government without approval by Parliament.

After his predecessor's debacle with national land rights, Gerry Hand still continued to issue challenges over land rights in State jurisdictions. In his 1987 policy statement, he said:

We make it clear once again that the Commonwealth will not allow situations to develop where a State or Territory can continue to evade its responsibilities. In this regard delay and deferral, or mere tokenism, are little different from outright refusal to act.[4]

The present Minister, Robert Tickner, has dropped such challenges, preferring to place his hope in State governments doing the right thing of their own accord. There is still a need for a national code of minimal behaviour for mining on Aboriginal land, enforceable by the Commonwealth Government, which exercises a discretion in the issuing of export licences. Mining companies should be required to obtain a certificate of approval from the Minister for Aboriginal Affairs before commencing mining operations on Aboriginal land.

The trigger for a national code providing minimal security of tenure and rights of control for land access will come with the Northern Territory's move to full statehood. If and when it becomes a State, it will inevitably take on legislative competence to deal with Aboriginal land in its jurisdiction. A change of government at a federal level would result in the Northern Territory legislature getting control of the Land Rights Act even before the grant of statehood. There is no reason why Aborigines in the Territory should lose any legislative protection they already enjoy. One condition of the patriation of the Commonwealth's Land Rights Act to the Territory Government will be continuing Commonwealth legislative safeguards of Aboriginal security, control and access to Aboriginal land. If such safeguards are to apply to Aborigines in one jurisdiction, then they should apply to Aborigines in all States. For the first time there will be the political will to institute a national code for Aboriginal land.

Culturally appropriate local government also needs to be provided for all Aboriginal communities who want it. Procedures under Commonwealth law for the protection of sacred sites need to be made more certain and less subject to ministerial discretion. Once the complexities of law and administration for land, local government, service delivery and sacred sites reflect the Aboriginal aspirations for recognition, belonging, participation and control, we will then be able to consider the collective political rights of Aborigines. In so doing there will be a need for a clear statement by government on the issues of sovereignty, self-determination and compensation.

Sovereignty as defined in international law and as understood by Australian parliamentarians is non-negotiable. For Aboriginal advocates, it is sterile ground for debate, unless there is to be a new definition of sovereignty. If it is to be a debate about semantics, it would be better focussed on terms such as autonomy and self-determination, within the Australian nation. Anything suggesting separate nation status for Aborigines living among other Australians in the streets of Redfern, or for those living on the outskirts of country towns like Mt Isa is just not on the agenda in Sydney, Canberra or even Geneva. The complexity, cost and confusion of such status might increase the power of some Aboriginal politicians. It is hard to see how it would increase Aboriginal control of their own lives. It would definitely result in an even more cumbersome bureaucracy, as local communities do not have sufficient skills or resources to provide for the delivery of their own services, except with the involvement of others who would then become foreign nationals. In any event, despite the claims of the Aboriginal Provisional Government's self-elected leaders, there is no groundswell of Aboriginal support for separate nation status.

Self-determination within the Australian nation is more than self-management and self-sufficiency. It is a fluid concept to be confined by the clear proviso that it is: 'subject to the Constitution and laws of the Commonwealth of Australia'. It encompasses less than the claim to separate nationhood. The claim to full-blown external self-determination will still be made by some Aboriginal advocates. Their claim cannot be explained away as Gerry Hand tried to do in 'Foundations for the Future':

There is a need to understand properly and to address seriously the vital issue of self-determination for Aboriginal and Islander people.

In the past there has been a misunderstanding of what Aboriginal people have meant when talking of self-determination. What has always existed is a willingness and desire by Aboriginal and Islander people to be involved in the decision-making process of government.

It is the right of Aboriginal and Islander people as citizens of this country to be involved in this process, as ultimately these decisions will affect their daily lives.[5]

It can be no consolation to advocates such as Michael Mansell to be told that they do not really understand the terminology they are using. They do understand all too well. It is just that what they advocate is not politically achievable and is not the only justifiable outcome for Aborigines in the light of two centuries of new occupation of this land. Assuming the moral legitimacy of the nation state in the international order, we must accept that national boundaries will enclose minorities and indigenous groups whose freedom of lifestyle and culture deserve to be respected. Indigenous groups should not be forced to be migrants in their own country, being integrated against their will into the new society. If unable to live apart, or even if they choose not to live apart, Aborigines should be able to live their own lives in the nation state with as much control as practicable over their own affairs. If that can be done, Aborigines and other Australians will constitute a nation that accords justice to Aborigines, though they do not live as a separate people. Though separate nation status is unachievable and (as I have dared to suggest) not desired by the majority of Aborigines today, this situation could change in decades to come for the people of the Torres Strait, or Arnhem Land, or the Central Desert, but I doubt it. Without a discrete territory and population base, other Aborigines will never have the option, it now being accepted in international law that, even in the context of decolonisation, 'the principle of territorial integrity generally preempts claims to self-determination with respect to people who reside within the frontiers of a sovereign state'.[6] There is nothing to be gained in the domestic nor international forum by pretending that Aborigines in Redfern or Fitzroy could ever live outside the frontiers of Australia while remaining in their homes, even if they wanted to define their reality that way. Ambit claims to separate nation status will gain nothing, except good press and hostility from vested interests. They will form no part even in the process, let alone in the outcome, of an instrument of reconciliation.

The contemporary world order has a legitimacy until we can replace it with one more centered on the rights and dignity of the individual, and the collective entitlement of discrete groups to free exercise of religion, culture and association. The present order has the nation state and its security and sovereignty as cornerstones. In that situation Aboriginal sovereignty, like that of the Irish clan of my forebears, has been eclipsed by the evolution of the nation state. Aboriginal claims to sovereignty would be more assured of success and on firmer moral ground if the emphasis were on greater autonomy for local communities within the Australian nation state, accompanied by reciprocal rights and duties by all seeking the common good.

There is no moral argument to say that any Aboriginal community, however small or dissipated it becomes, will forever or should forever be the owners of their traditional land. The creation is for the good and enjoyment of all. As Australians we have to face the fact that in an increasingly overcrowded world we retain exclusive use of too many of the world's resources. This is not to deny that Aborigines are at the bottom rung of the economic ladder in Australia nor that their ancestors were here first. And although we are a small population on a vast area of land, it is just and for the common good that our legal system make Aboriginal land as secure as it can be under our law, especially when that land is a spiritual as well as economic base for people needing space from a dominating colonial culture. There may be a time in the future when Australian land, Aboriginal and not, is justly made available for occupation and use by refugees or others fleeing overcrowding and death-dealing poverty. But in the moral calculus, Aboriginal claims to their land need to be recognised as being stronger than others. It is time that our legal system provided that recognition.

Presumably any national instrument of reconciliation is to be more than a symbolic acknowledgement of history with no legal or practical effect. Even if it were not to create new rights and duties between citizens distinguished on the basis of race, it may still grant Aborigines a collective entitlement to seek recourse against governments and their agents. Aborigines often claim that governments are too unfettered and insufficiently accountable in their political decisions regarding Aboriginal land rights and self-determination. In part, the reason is that these justifiable aspirations are not yet sufficiently recognised in Australian law, which has been built on the law of the colonisers.

Self-management and self-determination are not terms of legal precision. They are however aspirations of local Aboriginal communities wanting more control over their lives, culture and heritage. When Commonwealth Attorney-General, Mr R. J. Ellicott QC, referred the question of Aboriginal customary law to the Law Reform Commission, he took into account 'the right of Aborigines to retain their racial identity and traditional lifestyle or, where they so desire, to adopt partially or wholly a European lifestyle'.[7] Though this right might never become an enforceable legal right under local law, it should be viewed as what Justice Deane calls 'a moral entitlement to be treated in accordance with standards dictated by the fundamental notions of human dignity and essential equality which underlie the international recognition of human rights'.[8]

Aboriginal communities cheated of their moral entitle-ments need to be able to bring government to account in ways other than through swaying public opinion in the media or affecting government policy by political action.

The principles of self-management and self-determination should be governing principles applied with due discretion and ranked in priority with other social objectives reviewable by an arbiter.

Mr Tickner's chief initiative as Minister for Aboriginal Affairs has been the establishment of the Council for Aboriginal Reconciliation. The council is to facilitate the process of reconciliation and investigate the need for an instrument of reconciliation. The council will fail unless it recommends a workable legal device for ensuring the recognition and priority of Aboriginal rights and entitlements. At the very least, there should be a charter of Aboriginal recognition drawn up by 2001. There will be a need then for an Aboriginal recognition commission, which could review governmental action said to be in conflict with the charter. The commission would not undermine the sovereignty of parliaments nor trample upon the constraints on Federal and State powers. It could be like a Waitangi Tribunal but without the power to review actions before the date of its constitution. The Federal Opposition has been very critical of the 1985 changes to the Waitangi Tribunal for opening up 'the possibility of massive retrospective claims' and 'demands for vast tracts of crown land, for rights over the billion dollar New Zealand fishing industry, and for other privileges in a spirit of inverted racism'.[9]

A commission of at least seven members chaired by a prominent Australian needs to be set up by statute. The Government should consult with Aboriginal groups, the Opposition and State premiers about membership. The commission could employ staff to research and consult. It could host conferences and would be required annually to report to all governments through the Conference of Prime Minister and Premiers. Like a law reform commission or the Human Rights and Equal Opportunity Commission, it could invite submissions, hold public hearings and publish interim reports. The commission's annual report should be tabled in all parliaments.

Hopefully the Council for Aboriginal Reconciliation will be able to present a draft charter of aboriginal recognition to all governments at the Conference of Prime Minister and Premiers in 1999, allowing eighteen months for a referendum of approval. Ultimately the charter's contents would have to be put to the vote, not necessarily as a constitutional referendum but as a community endorsement of the fresh start.

Once approved and signed, the charter would be enforceable by Aborigines contesting policy, practice, or action of any government before the commission on the grounds that it contravened the charter. The commission would report its findings to the relevant parliament and could even be empowered to issue directions to ministers. Failing co-operation from a State government, the commission's role would be confined to Commonwealth matters within that State.

If we do not attempt to hammer out an agreement providing Aborigines with a secure foundation for living in Australia as they choose (though subject to the law), we will be left dependent on a legal regime that will have excluded forever the original Australians from the process of agreement to unite in one indissoluble Commonwealth. The present regime provides no permanent, assured, formal recognition of the continued entitlement of Aborigines to choose between their traditional lifestyle and that of other Australians. Without change, we will maintain the fictional character of the constitutional basis for our continued subjection of Aborigines to our laws without their consent now or at any time in the past.

If the charter proposal is unworkable, we should wait to hear that from Aborigines. If compromise is possible, Aborigines should be equipped to stand on an equal footing with government in a consultative process supervised by the Council for Aboriginal Reconciliation. Aboriginal participation in this process could be a real act of self-determination though admittedly subject to the now inescapable and sufficient qualification: 'subject to the Constitution and the laws of the Commonwealth of Australia'.

For some Aboriginal leaders, these suggestions will be very limp. But nothing more is politically conceivable. Even what has been put may not be politically achievable. Some Aboriginal leaders will continue pressing their claim that they are a separate nation state or series of nation states deserving international recognition and independence from their colonisers. No domestic arrangement between government and Australian citizens will satisfy them. Understandably they will see the proposed commission as flawed from the outset. It would be a serious mistake for them to hold out for nation status from the UN General Assembly. That will not be countenanced even by the Working Group on Indigenous Populations. Neither will their claims to self-determination be elevated to the claims of colonised people entitled to territorial partition. It will be for Aboriginal groups to determine whether they participate in the charter process. Government must provide the resources for local Aboriginal consultation as well as national discussions with leaders of peak Aboriginal bodies.

The charter of recognition could commence with the words: 'Whereas the people of Australia have agreed to live in one indissoluble Commonwealth . . .' Despite the utterances of some Aboriginal leaders, I suspect most Aborigines would agree if they were asked and if there followed words of mutual recognition and respect.

There would need to be an acknowledgement of human history in this land before 1788; acknowledgement of the effects of British settlement; and a recognition by the people of Australia of the Aboriginal entitlement, subject to the constitution and laws of the Commonwealth of Australia, to:

a) self-management and self-determination;
b) preservation and development of Aboriginal culture;
c) secure title to Aboriginal land which has not been alienated;

d) fair compensation for Aboriginal land alienated without consent after 1 January 2001;

e) protection of and control of access to sacred sites and sacred objects;

f) respect and support for Aboriginal languages, religion, law and history;

g) resolution of disputes under Aboriginal law or custom when all parties agree.

The process of formulation for the charter will contribute to a change in government and public consciousness. It will take time. The Canadian experience is illustrative. Their land claims settlements take years of consultations and negotiation. Their First Ministers' Conferences have failed to resolve the content of existing aboriginal rights that are recognised in the constitution. Over the years, however, they have put the issue on the national agenda and contributed to a more subtle understanding by the public that aboriginal rights are not an instance of unwarranted discrimination driving a wedge into the national identity, but of equal protection of the law providing a focus of national identity for peoples from diverse backgrounds and cultures.

Most Aborigines agitating for a treaty are not living on large remote areas where they are in the majority and may have much to gain commercially from resource agreements. Rather two-thirds of the Aboriginal population do not live as geographically discrete communities. They are a minority in cities and country towns, wanting recognition of their history and their place in the future of this country. They are Australian citizens; most want to remain so. But they do deserve greater assured recognition as the inheritors and custodians of the only culture unique to this land. Such recognition would consolidate the national identity of all Australians.

As well as any charter of collective rights for Aborigines, we need to acknowledge their place and rights in any revised constitution. In 1985, at the request of all State Parliaments, the Commonwealth Parliament passed the Australia Act that, as its preamble states, is 'An Act to bring the constitutional arrangements affecting the Commonwealth and the States into conformity with the status of the Commonwealth of Australia as a sovereign, independent and federal nation'. The Parliament and Government of the Commonwealth, with the concurrence of all the States then asked the Parliament of the United Kingdom to pass a similar Act, which it duly did. Prior to the Australia Acts, it was true to say, as had Sir Owen Dixon in 1935, that our constitution 'is not a supreme law purporting to obtain its force from the direct expression of a people's inherent authority to constitute a government. It is a statute of the British Parliament'.[10] Since the Australia Acts, it is arguable that the constitution 'now enjoys its character as a higher law because of the will and authority of the people'.[11] The signing and proclamation of the Charter of Aboriginal Recognition needs to be accompanied by the one act of national self-determination not achieved by the Australia Acts proclaimed in 1986 – the repatriation of our constitution from a schedule of an imperial Act to an expression of the national will of Australians in 2001. The constitution would then be the place to look for a brief preamble acknowledging the fullness of human history in this land and the special place of Aborigines in the Commonwealth of Australia. By then, we may have overcome the difficulties confronted by the Constitutional Commission in 1988 in trying to isolate 'the fundamental sentiments which Australians of all origins hold in common', and to state them in a concise and inspirational form.[12]

There needs to be a referendum for repatriation of the constitution in conjunction with the community endorsement of the Charter of Aboriginal Recognition. The preamble of the Australian Constitution Repatriation and Amendment Act 2001 could read:

Whereas the territory of Australia has long been occupied by Aborigines and Torres Strait Islanders whose ancestors inhabited Australia for thousands of years before British settlement:

And Whereas many Aborigines and Torres Strait Islanders suffered dispossession and dispersal upon exclusion from their traditional lands by the authority of the Crown:

And Whereas the people of Australia now include Aborigines, Torres Strait Islanders, migrants and refugees from many nations, and their descendants seeking peace, freedom, equality and good government for all citizens under the law:

And Whereas the people of Australia drawn from diverse cultures and races have agreed to live in one indissoluble Federal Commonwealth under the Constitution established a century ago and approved with amendment by the will of the people of Australia: Be it therefore enacted:

In the body of the constitution, there should be a clause recognising and affirming the existing rights of Aborigines and Torres Strait Islanders.

A charter of recognition backed by a tribunal with teeth, though subject to Parliament, complemented by a constitutional preamble stating the reality of our shared history and present identity as a nation, and constitutional recognition of Aboriginal rights could provide the basis for a just and proper settlement on a case by case basis. Having done what is possible to set right the legal wrongs of our past, we might succeed in establishing a legal order more able to give each his or her due, without fear or favour, regardless even of race.

Under the proposed charter, the Yarrabah Council after 1 January 2001 could put a case to the Aboriginal Recognition Commission and Senator Richardson's successors and their officers would be required to justify their decision for World Heritage Listing, taking account of the Aboriginal entitlement to self-management and self-determination. An adverse finding reported to Parliament would bring about a parliamentary review of the decision. The existence of this review process would provide Aboriginal communities with the opportunity to put their case for self-determination and would require government to justify publicly, policies that have insufficient regard for Aboriginal entitlements. Aborigines would be able to challenge the manner in which government departments deliver services in health, education and policing. Public servants would have to take account of the Aboriginal perspective.

Aboriginal aspirations for self-management and self-determination are not contrary to the common good of all Australians. Assimilation is not justice. Justice for the unassimilated requires recognition of their entitlements even in their distinctiveness. When in government in 1980, Senator Chaney said:

The concern which is felt by some Australians that the concept of a treaty involves the recognition of two nations, is a concern that the Government would wish to put to rest. The Government's approach to the treaty is this: We are not looking at two nations; we are looking at how the Australian nation properly deals with the situation of its Aboriginal people. If we can arrive at arrangements between the national Government and the Aboriginal people of Australia which are consensual in nature and which represent the view of Aboriginal citizens of this country as to what is appropriate, I believe we will have advanced.[13]

A bipartisan sponsorship of a charter of Aboriginal recognition is desirable and should be achievable. If not, the blame will lie with those politicians on both sides who abandon it or render it impossible because there is always an election in the air and those citizens who assume that assimilation is a pre-condition of justice for all. With an Aboriginal recognition commission we could build the bridge between the newcomers and their descendants and this land's traditional owners determining their future subject to the improved constitution and laws of the Commonwealth of Australia.

The Coalition parties' treatment of this issue when in government, the 1983 Senate Report and the 1988 Final Report of the Constitutional Commission provide a number of non-negotiable procedures for the process of consultation and education and non-negotiable parameters of the content of any legal instrument, if there is to be bipartisan support.

Non-negotiable procedures
1 State governments must be involved.
2 There must be an education and consultation process that includes non-Aborigines.
3 There must not be any artificial time constraint, though there may be a realistic target date of symbolic importance such as 1 January 2001, the centenary of the Australian constitution.
4 There must be no attempt at constitutional reform until the content of the instrument is finalised.
5 There needs to be a group of non-Aboriginal persons who are not politicians formally involved in the education, consultation and negotiation phases, as well as Aborigines and politicians.

Non-negotiable parameters
1 The document will not be a treaty in the international law sense.
2 There is no question of Aboriginal sovereignty separate from the sovereignty of the Commonwealth of Australia.
3 It will not be national land rights by the back door.
4 There will be recompense for past injustices in the form of special programmes for Aborigines but there will be no monetary compensation payable to Aborigines simply on the basis of race.
5 There will be no compensation payable for past deprivation of land, though there would be compensation payable for Aboriginal land acquired for public purposes after the date of the agreement.

6 There will be no compulsory acquisition of privately owned land.

7 There will be no interference with Federal-State relations, though there may be a legal machinery put in place for review of State and Commonwealth government decisions affecting Aborigines, if all State Governments so agree.

8 There will be no proposal for reserved Aboriginal seats in Parliament.

These restrictive parameters are implied in what Prime Minister Hawke has said on this issue since September 1987. They are confirmed by the Government's 1989 response to the Draft Declaration on the Rights of Indigenous Populations, and by the Government's statements in the Senate on the Coulter resolution. They highlight the modesty of the Hawke Government's proposals since 1987. Those proposals have been miscontrued by critics who have focussed on the international legal significance of the word 'treaty'.

Some Aborigines will reject any proposal that presumes Aborigines to be Australian citizens rather than citizens of a separate Aboriginal nation. Those of that view will be critical of anything attracting bipartisan support in this area. It is 200 years too late and at least 100 years too early for the constitutional arrangements they seek. Others see the need for symbolic action and an all-embracing policy, recognised in law, that respects the collective entitlement of Aborigines to self-management and self-determination, subject to the constitution and laws of the Commonwealth of Australia. These need to know the limits of what is negotiable.

If Aborigines were to seek more from the 'instrument of reconciliation' process, there would be a guaranteed loss of bipartisan support. If the government were to grant more than what is possible subject to these limits, that would require profound policy changes even by the Hawke Government.

Commitment to the process and instrument of reconciliation can be undertaken in good faith only if there are continuing efforts by governments and Aboriginal organisations to rectify the injustices resulting from years of neglect in the delivery of culturally appropriate social and welfare services. The instrument can be no replacement for secure land rights, effective local government and Aboriginal participation in government decision making that affects Aboriginal communities. It will not replace day-to-day priorities of community leaders; but it could provide a new lens through which those priorities will be perceived by government and the Australian community. This lens could replace what Professor Manning Clark described as the thick plate glass that has separated Aborigines and others on different sides, 'only able to see the grief and hatred on each other's faces, but not able to hear, let alone understand what was being said'.[14] Using all our senses to bridge the cultural gap, we must remember Professor Bill Stanner's reminder that those of us who are not Aboriginal are left 'tongueless and earless towards this other world of meaning and significance'.[15] The consultation process for the instrument of reconciliation should assist our hearing, understanding and seeing that other world of meaning, which has a claim to be recognised and protected by the instrument which results.

Under our developing legal system, we need to do more than provide the lens as an optional way of looking at the contemporary Aboriginal world. Government officials ought be required to use the lens whenever they deal with Aboriginal citizens. The spirit of the Barunga Statement might then take on meaning in the everyday lives of Aborigines and their organisations that are trying to address the pressing daily needs. Countering the twin evils of assimilation and discrimination, our lawmakers might then be able to assure Aborigines a place in Australian society, the only society in the world that owes a primary duty to Aborigines wanting to determine their future, by preserving and developing their culture. None of this necessarily entails separate nations of black and white; nor does it demand financial payments of compensation to individuals simply on the basis of race.

The Barunga Statement was signed by two traditional elders in the Northern Territory. Each of them espoused the need for a treaty within one Australia, what the other signatories Mr Hawke and Mr Hand and their fellow ministers now call an instrument of reconciliation. Approaching the first centenary of our existence as a federation under the constitution, we have the time to negotiate a just and proper settlement. Committed to finding common ground, we need to settle so that no Australian is alien to the land or to the society that is our common heritage. We might then share the country with all belonging to this land.

If only our Aboriginal and non-Aboriginal leaders could be convinced that it is time to 'talk strong', the curse could be lifted from Tjurkurpa. The house on Capital Hill could be seen as the highest meeting place in the land – for all Australians, even the first Australians. And Mr Tjakamarra might be heard by all Australians: 'I designed Tjurkurpa for a good purpose, for both black and white.' Agreement could make every Australian's place strong in this land.

Notes

Introduction

1   Canberra Times, 11 May 1988
2   (1990) CPD 8 (Senate); 8 May 1990
3   A.S. Peacock to author, letter, 28 November 1989
4   Letter to author, 28 November 1989
5   R. J. Hawke, 'A Time for Reconciliation', in A Treaty With Aborigines?, Institute of Public Affairs, 1988, p. 4
6   J. Howard, 'Treaty is a Recipe for Separatism', in A Treaty With Aborigines?, p. 7
7   Hawke, 'A Time for Reconciliation', p. 5
8   W. E. H. Stanner, White Man Got No Dreaming, ANU Press, Canberra, 1979, p. ix
9   Land Rights News, vol. 2, no. 9, July 1988, p. 24

Chapter 1

1   *Cooper* v *Stuart* (1889) 14 AC at p. 291.
2   *Coe* v *The Commonwealth and the Government of the United Kingdom of Great Britain and Northern Ireland* (1979) 53 ALJR 403 at p. 409
3   *Western Sahara Case* (1975) ICJ 12 at p. 42
4   Ibid., p. 49
5   Ibid., p. 53
6   Ibid., p. 68
7   (1978)52 ALJR 334 at p. 336
8   (1979)53 ALJR 403 at pp. 408–9

9   Ibid., p. 410

10 (1975)ICJ 12 at p. 39

11 *Milirrpum* v *Nabalco Pty Ltd* (1971) 17 FLR 141 at p. 198

12 Ibid., pp. 147, 198, 244, 245, 247, 252, 262, 273, 274; and see Brennan J.,
    Re Toohey, Ex parte Meneling Station (1982) 44 ALR 63 at p. 85.

13 (1971) 17 FLR 141 at p. 223, referring to the decision of Gould J in
    Calder v *Attorney-General of British Columbia* (1969) 8 DLR (3rd) p. 59

14 *Calder et al* v *Attorney General of British Columbia* (1973) 34 DLR (3rd)
    145 at p. 218

15 *Coe* v *Commonwealth* (1978) 52 ALJR 334 at p. 408

16 (1978) 52 ALJR 334 at p. 412

17 Ibid., p. 411

18 K. McNeil, *Common Law Aboriginal Title*, Clarendon Press, Oxford, 1989,
    p. 298

19 Prof. R. D. Lumb, 'Is Australia an Occupied or Conquered Country?',
    Queensland Bar News, December 1984, p. 19.

20 (1971) 17 FLR 141, at p. 267 (Blackburn J)

21 *Queensland Coast Islands Declaratory Act 1985*, ss. 3 & 5

22 Hon. W. Gunn, (1985) QPD 4741; 2 April 1985

23 *Gerhardy* v *Brown* (1985) 57 ALR 472 at p. 532.

24 *Mabo* v *Queensland* (1988) 83 ALR 14 at p. 29 (Brennan, Toohey and
    Gaudron JJ)

25 (1988) 83 ALR 14 at p. 40 (Deane J)

26 Ibid., p. 34 (Brennan, Toohey and Gaudron JJ)

27 *Aboriginal Land Rights (Northern Territory) Act 1976*, s. 3(1)

28 (1971) 17 FLR 141 at p. 167, (Blackburn J)

29 See 'Discussion between Sir Edward Woodward, Dr N. Petersen and
    Professor M. Charlesworth', Deakin University, p. 24.

30 (1982) 44 ALR 63 at p. 87.

31 P. Seaman QC, *Aboriginal Land Inquiry*, September 1984, Government
    Printer, Western Australia, p. 11.

32 (1985) 57 ALR 472 at pp. 521–2

33 *Minister for Aboriginal Affairs* v *Peko Wallsend* (1986) 66 ALR 299 at p. 305

34 (1965) 48 CPD 2639 (H of R)

35 (1967) 54 CPD 263 (H of R)

36 Commonwealth Electoral Office, *Referendum Proposals*, 1967, p. 11

37 (1983) 46 ALR 625 at p. 791

38 Ibid., p. 816

39 W. E. H. Stanner, *White Man Got No Dreaming*, ANU Press, Canberra, 1979, pp. 300–1

40 Ibid., p. 357

41 UN Resolution 1514 (XV), s. 2, 14 December 1960, GAOR, 15th session, supp. 16, p. 66

42 Ibid., s. 6

43 (1975) ICJ 12 at p. 33

44 (1989) CPD 663 (Senate), 31 August 1989

45 (1987) 158 CPD 3153 (H of R)

46 P. Donnelly, address to Aboriginal and Islander Catholic Council, Rockhampton, 9 January 1990

47 International Union for Conservation of Nature and Natural Resources, World Heritage Bureau, 12th Ordinary Session, Documentation on World Heritage Properties (Natural), Paris, June 1988, p. 11

48 Aboriginal Co-ordinating Council, annual report, 1988-89, p. 12

49 Perron to Hawke, letter, 19 March 1990

50 Ministerial statement, 1 May 1990, pp. 12–15

51 *Hansard*, 1 May 1990, pp. 40–2

52 Hewson to Hawke, letter, 22 June 1990

53 Colleen Costello and Dennis Walker to Archbishop Rush, letter and enclosures, Brisbane, 8 June 1989

Chapter 2

1 (1975) 63 CPD (Senate) 367, 20 February 1975

2 Much of the history of the treaty idea until 1983 when the Aboriginal Treaty Committee disbanded is contained in two books by its members Stewart Harris, *It's Coming Yet*, Aboriginal Treaty Committee, Canberra, 1979, and Judith Wright, *We Call for a Treaty*, Collins/Fontana, Sydney, 1985

3 *Bulletin*, 2 August 1988

4 CAAC to NAC, letter, 29 July 1980

5 Wright, *We Call for a Treaty*, p. 125

6 (1981) 88 CPD 713 (Senate)

7   (1981) 88 CPD 878 (Senate)

8   Senate Standing Committee on Constitutional and Legal Affairs, *Hansard*, 22 June 1982, Canberra, p. 626

9   Ibid., p. 638

10   Ibid., p. 652

11   I. Wilson, 'The Makarrata and the Government', *Aboriginal Law Bulletin*, no. 5, August 1982, p. 5

12   Australian Labor Party Platform, Constitution and Rules as approved by the 36th National Conference, Canberra, 1984, *Aboriginals and Islanders*, p. 2.

13   (1983) 98 CPD 459 (Senate)

14   *Two Hundred Years Later*, report by the Senate Standing Committee on Constitutional and Legal Affairs, AGPS, Canberra, 1983, p. 50

15   Ibid., p. 115

16   Ibid., p. 162

17   (1983) 99 CPD 597 (Senate)

18   (1983) 100 CPD 1746 (Senate)

19   (1983) 134 CPD 3485 (H of R)

20   Ibid., p. 3493

21   Ibid., p. 3487

22   Ibid., p. 3489

23   Prime Minister's press conference, transcript, 19 October 1984, p. 2.

24   Ibid.

25   (1985) 109 CPD 2961 (Senate)

26   C. Holding, news release, 13 August 1985

27   (1985) 145 CPD 2771 (H of R)

28   (1985) 145 CPD 4247 (H of R)

29   (1986) 148 CPD 1473 (H of R)

30   Ibid.

31   Ibid., p. 1475

32   (1986) 152 CPD 3719 (H of R)

33   Ibid.

34   Hawke to Holding, letter, quoted in *Centralian Advocate*. 22 May 1987

35   National Press Club, address, 27 May 1987

36   Hawke, press conference, 2 September 1987

37   S. Tipaloura, media release, 3 August 1987

38   1987 *Hansard*, (N.T.), 1620; 24 September 1987

39   *Bulletin*, 22 September 1987, pp. 20, 23
40   (1987) 122 CPD 6 (Senate)
41   (1987) 156 CPD 861-2 (H of R)

Chapter 3

1   press release, 13 June 1988
2   *Catholic Leader*, 24 January 1988, p. 10
3   (1988) 162 CPD 140 (H of R)
4   (1988) 162 CPD 137 (H of R); (1988) 128 CPD 56 (Senate), 23 August
     1988
5   (1987) 158 CPD 3162 (H of R)
6   (1988) 162 CPD 139 (H of R)
7   Ibid., p. 138
8   Ibid., p. 139
9   Quoted at (1988) 128 CPD 71 (Senate), 23 August 1988
10   F. M. Chaney and I. Viner, "An Accommodation of Interests", 1980, p. 5
11   *Distribution of Powers*, Report of the Advisory Committee to the
     Constitutional Commission, AGPS, Canberra, 1987, p. 104
12   Ibid., p. 117
13   Ibid.
14   Ibid.
15   R. J. Hawke, 'A Time for Reconciliation', in *A Treaty With Aborigines?*,
     Institute of Public Affairs, 1988, pp. 4–5
16   J. Howard, 'Treaty Is A Recipe for Separatism', ibid., p. 6–7
17   G. Yunupingu, 'Why a Treaty?' in ibid., pp. 6–7
18   R. Liddle, 'Aborigines are Australian, too', ibid., p. 14
19   'Aboriginal Sovereignty', *Aboriginal Law Bulletin*, vol. 2, no. 37, April
     1989, pp. 5–6
20   Prime Minister's News Conference, transcript, Auckland, 2 February
     1990
21   *Land Rights News*, vol. 2, no. 18, February 1990, p. 7
22   1989 CPD 1326 (H of R); 11 April 1989
23   1989 CPD 2734 (H of R); 24 May 1989
24   Ibid.

25 (1988) 162 CPD 253 (H of R); 24 August 1988. Repeated at (1989) CPD 1997 (H of R); 4 May 1989

26 (1987) 158 CPD 3198 (H of R)

27 *Aboriginal Land (Lake Condah and Framlingham Forest) Act* 1987 and the principal Act amended by the *Aboriginal and Torres Strait Islander Heritage Protection Amendment Act* 1987

28 1989 CPD 2016 (Senate); 17 October 1989

29 Ibid.

30 1989 CPD 105 (Senate); 16 August 1989

31 1989 CPD 2022 (Senate); 17 October 1989

32 R. J. Hawke to J. Coulter, letter, quoted in J. Coulter's media release, 18 December 1989

33 (1989) CPD1973-4 (Senate); 17 October 1989

34 Interview with Cherie Pryor, transcript, TAIMA, 23 November 1989

35 news conference, transcript, Auckland, 2 February 1990

36 news conference, transcript, Brisbane, 9 March 1990

37 Liberal Party policy statement, 1990, p. 18

38 National Party policy statement, 1990, pp. 34-5

39 *Age,* 23 March 1990

40 ibid.

41 Hawke to Hewson, letter, 7 May 1990

42 Hewson to Hawke, letter, 22 June 1990

43 (1989) CPD 666 (Senate); 31 August 1989

44 Hewson to Hawke, letter, 20 June 1990

45 *Australian,* 13 October 1989

46 (1989) CPD 2019 (Senate); 17 October 1989

47 *Age,* 28 June 1990

48 *Age,* 28 June 1990

49 *Weekend Australian,* 30 June 1990

50 *Australian,* 29 June 1990

51 *Weekend Australian,* 30 June 1990

52 Cooper to Hawke, letter, 31 May 1990

53 L. O'Donoghue, 'Immigration and Australia's Aboriginal Communities', *Bureau of Immigration Research Conference,* Melbourne, 15 November 1990, p. 9

54 *Backgrounder,* Department of Foreign Affairs and Trade, vol. 1, no. 32, 3 December 1990, p. 6

55   *Land Rights News*, vol. 2, no. 9, July 1988, p. 25

Chapter 4

1   UN Economic and Social Council, E/CN.4/Sub.2/1986/7/Add.4, pp. 42–3

2   E/CN.4/Sub.2/AC.4/1983/2/Add.2, p. 3

3   Resolution 1984/35B

4   E/CN.4/Sub.2/1985/22/Annex III, p. 1

5   E/CN.4/Sub.2/1985/22/Annex IV, p. 1

6   E/CN.4/Sub.2/AC.4/1988/2, p. 9

7   E/CN.4/Sub.2/AC.4/1988/5, p. 9

8   E/CN.4/Sub.2/AC.4/1988/2/Add.1, p. 5

9   Ibid., pp. 78–9.

10 The Australian Government Response to the Draft Declaration on the Rights of Indigenous Populations, Document E/CN.4/Sub.2/1989/33; 15 June 1989

11 S. Houston, 'Capturing the Clouds', *Aboriginal Law Bulletin*, 1989, vol. 2, no. 40, p. 6.

12 Opening statement of Australian Government delegation, ILO conference, 76th session, June 1989, agenda item IV

13 Article 1(3).

14 E/CN.4/Sub.2/AC.4/1989/3/Add.2, p. 5

15 Geoff Clarke, National Coalition of Aboriginal Organisations, statement at ILO conference 1988, *Aboriginal Law Bulletin*, no. 34, p. 13.

16 'Aboriginal Peoples and Treaties', seminar report, Aboriginal Law Centre, University of New South Wales, 1989, p. 28.

17 Geoff Clarke, 'ILO convention 197 – Revision or Reversion?', *Aboriginal Law Bulletin*, no. 40, 1989 p. 4

18 E/CN.4/Sub.2/1989/36, p. 10

19 Eagleton, 'Excesses of Self-Determination', in *Foreign Affairs* no. 31, 1953, 592 at p. 602

Chapter 5

1   Jane Kelsey, 'The Treaty of Waitangi Tribunal and Maori Independence – Future Directions', 9th Commonwealth Law Conference, Auckland 1990, p. 249

2   *Hoani Te Heuheu* v *Aotea District Maori Land Board* (1941) AC 308 at p. 324

3   *New Zealand Maori Council* v *Attorney General* [1987] 1 NZLR 641 at pp. 664, 719

4   Ibid., p. 664

5   Report of the Waitangi Tribunal on the Mangonui Sewerage Claim, WAI-17 (1988) p. vii

6   *Mahuta and Tainui Trust Board* v *Attorney General* (unreported, Court of Appeal, 3 October 1989)

7   *Sydney Morning Herald*, 16 June 1990

8   *Mahuta and Tainui Trust Board* v *Attorney General* ibid.

9   Royal Proclamation of 1763, RSC 1970, app. II, no.1, at p. 128

10 (1973) 34 DLR (3rd) p. 145

11 Ibid., p. 156

12 Ibid., p. 218 (Spence and Larkin JJ concurring)

13 The five agreements are the James Bay (1975) and North Eastern Quebec (1978) agreements and in the territories, the Inuvialuit (COPE)(1983), the Dene and Metis (1988) and the Tungavik Federation of Nunavut (1990) agreements

14 Information submitted by the Government of Canada to the UN Working Group on Indigenous Populations, E/CN.4/Sub.2/AC.4/1989/2, p. 11

15 (1985) 13 DLR (4th) 321

16 Ibid., p. 335

17 Ibid., p. 339 (Beetz, Chouinard and Lamer JJ concurring)

18 Ibid., p. 341

19 Ibid., p. 356 (Ritchie and McIntyre JJ concurring)

20 *Canadian Pacific Ltd* v *Paul* (1988) 2 SCR 654 at p. 677

21 'Canada: Towards Aboriginal Self-Government?', in *A Treaty With the Aborigines?*, Institute of Public Affairs, K. Baker (ed.), 1988, 32 at p. 35

22 Quoted in D. Sanders, 'Canada: The First Ministers' Conferences on Aboriginal Rights', *Aboriginal Law Bulletin* 8, no. 27, 1987, at p. 9

23 Special Committee to Study the Proposed Companion Resolution to the Meech Lake Accord, *Report*, May 1990, p. 11

24 D. Hawkes quoted by G. Nettheim in 'Canadian Studies – Review', *Aboriginal Law Bulletin*, no. 22, 1986, p. 10

Conclusion

1 Senate Standing Committee on Constitutional and Legal Affairs, *Official Hansard Report*, Alice Springs, 29 March 1982, p. 266

2 Ibid., pp. 268-9

3 W. Gray quoted by R. Barsh, 'Revision of ILO Convention 107', in *American Journal of International Law*, no. 81, 1987, 756 at p. 761

4 *Foundations for the Future*, AGPS, 1988, pp. 5-6

5 Ibid., p. 1

6 S. K. N. Blay, 'Self-Determination versus Territorial Integrity in Decolonization', *International Law and Politics* no. 18,1986, 441 at p. 472

7 *ALRC* no. 31, vol. 1, p. xxxv (terms of reference, 9 February 1977)

8 *Mabo* v *Queensland* (1988) 83 ALR 14 at p. 42

9 (1989) CPD (Senate) 572; 30 August 1989 (Senator Knowles)

10 Sir Owen Dixon, 'The Law and the Constitution', *Law Quarterly Review*, no. 51, 1935, 590 at p. 597

11 G. J. Lindell, 'Why is Australia's Constitution Binding?' *Federal Law Review* no. 16, 1986, 29 at p. 37

12 Constitutional Commission, final report, vol. 1, p. 109

13 Quoted by G. Hand, (1988) 162 CPD pp. 150, 823

14 C. M. H. Clark, *A Discovery of Australia*, ABC Publications, Sydney, 1976, p. 23

15 W. E. H. Stanner, 'After the Dreaming' in *White Man Got No Dreaming*, ANU Press, Canberra, 1979, p. 230

Don't Take Your Love to Town   Ruby Langford

Ruby Langford was born on Bos Ridge mission, Coraki, on the north coast of NSW in 1934. She was raised in Bonalbo, and went to high school in Casino where she finished second form. At age 15 she moved to Sydney and became a qualified clothing machinist. Her first child was born when she was 17. She has a family of nine children and raised them mostly by herself. For many years she lived in tin huts and camped in the bush around Coonabarabran, working at fencing, burning off, ringbarking and lopping, and pegging kangaroo skins. At other times she lived in the black areas of Sydney, and worked in clothing factories. She now works part-time at the Aboriginal Medical Service in Redfern, and is the grandmother of eighteen children.

'If you pick up this book, you pick up a life. It is as simple and as difficult as that. The life Langford has lived in Australia is as close to the eyes and ears as print on the page makes it.'

Billy Marshall-Stoneking, *Australian*

Recovery   Charles Rowley

In *Recovery*, Charles Rowley shares his knowledge of the background to the debate on Aboriginal land rights and welfare payments; shares his concern that the current backlash against Aboriginal claims is rooted in self-interest and prejudice; and shares his compassionate vision with a program – and a plea for Aboriginal recovery from the depredation and degradation of the past.

BOOKS BY HENRY REYNOLDS:

The Other Side of the Frontier

Using documentary and oral evidence, much of it previously unpublished, Henry Reynolds sets out the Aboriginal reactions to the coming of the Europeans to Australia. Contrary to conventional beliefs the Aborigines were not passive: they resorted to guerilla warfare, sorcery, theft of white settlers' goods, crops and animals, retribution and revenge sallies, and the adaptation of certain of the newcomers' ways. In presenting this material, Reynolds challenges us to reconsider not only our interpretation of our history, but also the implications for future relations between the peoples of Australia.

'Reynolds has painted an exciting and compelling picture of . . . resistance seen from the Aboriginal side . . . in most cases Aborigines fought heroically against overwhelming odds and superior weapons to resist usurpation of their lands, their rights and their livelihood.'

Age Monthly Review

BOOKS BY HENRY REYNOLDS: (Cont'd)

The Law of the Land

'I am at a loss to conceive by what tenure we hold this country, for it does not appear to be that we either hold it by conquest or by right of purchase.'

G. A. Robinson, 1832

In this readable and dramatic book, Henry Reynolds reassesses the legal and political arguments used to justify the European settlement of Australia. His conclusions form a compelling case for the belief that the British government conceded land rights to the Aborigines early in the nineteenth century.

With the White People

Guides, linguists, diplomats, interpreters, trackers, troopers, servants, companions, labourers, concubines, nursemaids, cooks, stockworkers, porters, pearl-divers, mine-workers.

The fascinating story of Australia's black pioneers has been largely overlooked by both black and white commentators.

Henry Reynolds' book *The Other Side of the Frontier* was described as 'the most important book ever on Aboriginal-European contact'. *With the White People* now provides a challenging reinterpretation of the role of those blacks whose efforts were vital to the development of colonial Australia.

Dreamtime Nightmares Bill Rosser

The early settlers in Northern Australia, building their extensive stations, were short of labour – until they discovered the ability of the Aboriginal men and women as stockriders.

'There is Jack Punch, who in the wink of an eye could revert to his tribal lifestyle, if given the chance . . . Harry Spencer did not know the white man's word until he was a man. Poor Harry! When he first saw sheep he thought they were Shetland ponies . . . Peggy James and Dorothy Webster are two tribal women in dresses and shoes. Usually laconic, it is only when they talk about the "old times" that their fat cheeks crease with a smile, even though "Those times was bloody crook, mate".'

It is Bill Rosser's unique talent of setting the scene and then teasing out the life stories of fellow Aboriginal women and men which makes *Dreamtime Nightmares* such a compelling book.